Being Heard

Being Heard

The Experiences of Young Women in Prostitution

Edited by Kelly Gorkoff and Jane Runner

Fourth in the Hurting and Healing Series on Intimate Violence

Co-published by Fernwood Publishing and
RESOLVE **(Research and Education for Solutions to Violence and Abuse)**

Editing: Eileen Young
Cover image: Getty Images
Design and production: Beverley Rach
Printed and bound in Canada

second printing January 2006

A publication of Fernwood Publishing
Site 2A, Box 5, 32 Oceanvista Lane
Black Point, Nova Scotia, B0J 1B0
and 324 Clare Avenue
Winnipeg, Manitoba, R3L 1S3
www.fernwoodbooks.ca
and RESOLVE (Research and Education for Solutions to Violence and Abuse)
108 Isbister Building, University of Manitoba
Winnipeg, Manitoba, R3T 2N2

Fernwood Publishing Company Limited gratefully acknowledges the financial support of the Department of Canadian Heritage, the Nova Scotia Department of Tourism and Culture and the Canada Council for the Arts for our publishing program.

National Library of Canada Cataloguing in Publication

Being heard: the experiences of young women in prostitution /
edited by Kelly Gorkoff and Jane Runner.

(Hurting and healing series)
Includes bibliographical references.
ISBN 1-55266-101-6

1. Prostitution—Canada.   I. Gorkoff, Kelly, 1965-   II. Runner, Jane III. Series.

HQ148.B43 2003   306.74'2'0971   C2003-900128-8

Contents

Dedication

It is clear from our interviews with women and men that life on the street is often not a happy one. It is one ridden with violence, abuse, humiliation, stigma, and pain. However, in the midst of adversity lies strength. The participants in this study were proud and formidable. Their integrity and bravery needs to be celebrated. In addition, the people with whom we spoke who work with such youth also displayed strength, passion, and patience in what is often a little rewarded and highly frustrating sector. It is to them that we dedicate this book.

Acknowledgments

We gratefully acknowledge the support of RESOLVE for this volume and its commitment to producing this series of research-based volumes. We also recognize the support of the Hurting and Healing series publication committee.

We recognize Status of Women Canada for funding "The Girl Child" research project. As well, we acknowledge the other members of the Alliance of Five Research Centres on Violence for their academic and collegial support. Since the project reported on here was a community academic effort, we thank the advisory committees representing several agencies in both Winnipeg and Calgary for their guidance and direction throughout the project. We thank all the research assistants and transcribers, as well as office and administrative support. Although not a contributing author to this volume, we recognize the research work of Jane Ursel as a member of the research team. Most importantly, this research could not have been done if not for the individual participants who boldly and bravely shared their stories with us and who have allowed us to use their experiences to learn more about this issue.

There are a number of individuals who assisted us at various stages throughout this book. We wish to thank our anonymous reviewer who provided feedback on the entire manuscript. We are especially grateful for the guidance and direction of Wayne Antony of Fernwood Publishing. Also, thanks to Eileen Young for editing the final manuscript, Beverley Rach for design and production, Brenda Conroy for proofreading and Debbie Mathers for inputting the final manuscript.

About the Authors

KAREN BUSBY, LL.B., LL.M., is a teacher, researcher and lawyer specializing in issues related to law and sex, sexual violence and sexuality. She is a professor of law at the University of Manitoba. She has worked with numerous community organizations, including rape crisis centres, the Women's Legal Education and Action Fund (LEAF), Group Organizing on Same Sex Issues and Principles (GOSSIP) and RESOLVE.

PAMELA J. DOWNE, Ph.D., is an associate professor of Women's and Gender Studies at the University of Saskatchewan. As a medical anthropologist, her work has focused on issues of health among marginalized women, including those women involved in local and global systems of prostitution. Most recently, her interests are in medical and community constructions of violence, fatigue and brain injury.

KELLY GORKOFF, M.A., is a former research associate at RESOLVE Manitoba and a lecturer in the Sociology Department at the University of Manitoba. Her research focus is on social programming and policy with a specific interest in political economy issues as they pertain to youth. She is currently undertaking her doctorate work in the Department of Sociology and Anthropology at Carleton University.

KENDRA NIXON, M.S.W., is the Community Research Development Coordinator for RESOLVE Alberta, a tri-prairie research institute on violence and abuse. Her research interests include woman abuse and social policy. Kendra has worked as a counsellor for battered women and as a child protection worker.

JANE RUNNER is the Program Manager for the Transition, Education and Resources for Females (TERF) program of New Directions, an organization in Winnipeg, Manitoba. TERF provides a culturally appropriate and supportive healing environment for women and transgender individuals ages thirteen and up who have been exploited through the sex trade. Jane has been advocating for seventeen years, both locally and nationally, for the rights of individuals exploited through the sex trade. She was instrumental in the development of P.O.W.E.R. (Prostitutes and Other Women for Equal Rights) in Winnipeg. Jane is a YWCA Woman of Distinction and has rightfully earned many accolades for her tireless work.

LESLIE TUTTY, Ph.D., is a full professor with the Faculty of Social Work at the University of Calgary, where she teaches courses in both clinical social work methods and research. Her research focus over the past fifteen years has been violence prevention and treatment for those affected by intimate partner violence. This includes evaluations of school-based prevention programs and interventions for those affected by family violence such as evaluations of shelter and post-shelter programs for abused women, support groups for abused women, treatment for adult and child victims of sexual abuse and groups for men who abuse their partners. Currently on leave for one year, she has served as the Academic Research Co-ordinator of RESOLVE Alberta since 1999.

MEGHAN WATERS is a crisis worker with the Youth Emergency Stabilization Team in Winnipeg. She has been a private personal coun-sellor and worked with children and youth in a variety of settings. She participated in the "Girl Child" research project at RESOLVE, acting as a counsellor for the women and men whom we were interviewing.

Introduction
Children and Youth Exploited through Prostitution

Kelly Gorkoff with Jane Runner

For over fifteen years now, Canadian research has been conducted on children and youth involved in prostitution. Numerous things have taken place in that time. We have expanded and confirmed our knowledge about certain aspects of this complex social issue, we have asked new questions, we have changed terminology, we have engaged in new debates, and we have introduced some innovative (albeit controversial) social programs and policy initiatives. However, even within this recently developed knowledge and practice, there exist many misconceptions and different perspectives on conceptualizing youth prostitution. Questions and answers fly from feminists, non-feminists, sex-trade workers, advocates, concerned citizens, service providers, mothers, fathers, youth, government bureaucrats—the list goes on. Within these differing points of view it is easy to become lost. The goal of this volume is to view the issue by hearing the voices of those involved, as a way to clarify important issues, dispel myths and misconceptions, and challenge conventional views of young women who sell sex.

Prostitution and Youth—How Do They Fit? Definition/Terminology

Prostitution has historically been deemed a moral crime. The so-called "world's oldest profession" has a precarious position in society. Prostitution has generally been tolerated as something that invariably exists, as something that happens with regularity and some degree of normalcy. Prostitution, while never fully accepted, is not fully rejected. It is rather condoned as a "necessary evil" by most segments of society. This precariousness is encapsulated in our legislation. Although the practice of prostitution is legal in Canada, solicitation and other activities associated with the act of prostitution are illegal.

The debate on how to conceptualize prostitution has taken place primarily in the feminist literature concerning adult women. Broadly speaking, there are two sides to the debate. Generally, the "feminist perspective" holds that the existence prostitution is an expression of male domination, through which women are commodified and exploited. Debates from this perspective frame the issue in the discourse of victimization and exploitation. They argue that prostitution is yet another site of inequality, degradation, dehumanization and the objectification of women (MacKinnon 1987; Dworkin 1988). Thus, embedded in the solution to end female inequality is a commitment to eradicate prostitution on the grounds that it oppresses and harms women. While most who support this perspective agree that prostitution should be eradicated, they do not support the criminalization of prostitution. Rather, they support de-criminalization as support for working women until underlying conditions can be changed. The other side of the debate, loosely termed "pro-sex-work feminism," critiques the general feminist contention by arguing that women must redefine their experience with sex and embrace all definitions and experiences of women's sexuality. Rather than victimizing, in certain historical times and places, prostitution empowers women financially and socially, as well as personally and politically, and allows women to interpret sex for themselves (McElroy 1997). Thus, sex work is, in principle, considered legitimate work, not violence (Vanwesenbeeck 2001: 243).

It is important to note that neither of these perspectives focuses directly on the experience of youth, although both indirectly implicate girls. This is a recognized gap in the feminist prostitution literature, namely theorizing about youth involved in the sex trade. Youth and adult sex-trade work is traditionally separated in both research and theory. The issue of youth is primarily addressed through the lens of examining street youth and child abuse, and is focused on the abhorrent and abusive nature of the act. Over the past two decades there has been a growing assertion among concerned parties that this activity on the part of children and youth is better viewed as distinct from adult prostitution. Rather, utilizing the framework of child abuse of a sexual and commercial nature is increasingly seen as the most appropriate way to describe this activity. This viewpoint was given more legitimacy with the publication of the Badgley report in 1984, which considered youth prostitution to be sexual abuse of a young person rather than a case of delinquency by a youth. This attitude is prevalent today. Out from the Shadows and into the Light, an ongoing national project operated by experiential (former sex-trade involved) youth devoted to the prevention of youth prostitution, put it this way:

> The term child or youth prostitute can no longer be used. These children and youth are sexually exploited and any language or reference to them must reflect that belief. We declare that the commercial sexual exploitation of children and youth is a form of child abuse and slavery. (Bramly et al. 1998: 8)

This notion of youth prostitution as abuse is clearly reflected in our laws and the legal discourse. The *Criminal Code* is indeed a major site of separation of youth from adult prostitution. Legal indicators include the elements of the *Criminal Code of Canada* that specifically address youth prostitution, particularly section 212(2), procuring or living on the avails of a person under eighteen years of age, and section 212(4), attempting to purchase or purchasing sex from persons under eighteen (see also Dawson 1987; Lowman 1987, 1998, 2000; Federal/Provincial/Territorial Working Group 1998; Alberta Task Force Report, 1997). Whether these legal approaches are effective in protecting children is a topic of considerable debate (see Lowman 2000; Bittle 2002). There have been few arrests and fewer convictions. As Lowman argues (1998), youth are reluctant to testify because they would not want to alienate their potential sources of income, and are intimidated by the process of having to appear in court. Thus, these laws may compromise independence and autonomy of youth.

More generally speaking, separating youth from adult sex-trade work is necessary to unveil important issues that uniquely impact youth. In separating, one can reveal that youth experience the social world (as a labourer, as a citizen, through culture) in distinct ways from adults. Thus, their experience of sex trade involvement will also be different.

However, others argue that it may be counter-productive to separate adult and youth prostitution because the process of prostitution and the life circumstances of those involved do not differ solely or perhaps even largely according to age. Many advocates for prostitute rights suggest that separating youth from adult prostitutes is inadequate because, in doing so, the contextual nature of prostitution is lost, situating youth purely as victims who need to be saved.[1] Research has clearly indicated that the circumstances that bring youth and adults to sex-trade work and keep them there are more similar than different. In addition, the experiences of sex work are similar. Thus, some researchers suggest it is confusing and potentially non-constructive to study youth prostitution as child abuse alone. As Brannigan and Fleischman argued in 1989, researching and intervening from this mutually exclusive stance are potentially incompatible. For example, is it realistic and effective to treat youth as victims and adults as non-victims? What does that mean to a seventeen-year-old youth prostitute? Will she have access to social service supports for one year as a victim of child abuse, then become a public nuisance? Another difficulty in researching youth prostitution exclusively through the lens of victim and abuse is that issues concerning the experience of sex work for youth are left unexamined. A relatively high number of research studies have focused on adult prostitution's working routines and how risk, stress and identity are managed (see Vanwesenbeeck 2001 for a review). Not examining work-related issues, such as how youth sex-trade workers manage their work and risk, and the way they cope with stressful demands, may unintentionally harm the health and safety of youth sex-trade workers. By casting the net in terms of victimization, one runs the risk of entrenching stigma and pushing girls further and further away from supports. Thus, viewing youth prostitutes solely as victims both legislatively and theoretically may be problematic.

What Is the Sexual Exploitation of Youth and Children?

Although there is no completely typical experience of youth and children involved in prostitution, there are some commonalities that are consistently expressed in research. Research in the past twenty years has focused on defining who youth prostitutes are and why they enter prostitution.

The definition of sexual exploitation is best conceptualized on a continuum. It ranges from female sexual slavery (the gorilla pimp) to survival sex (sale of sexual services by persons, such as homeless youth and women in poverty, who have very few other options) through to the more bourgeois styles of sex trade (including some street prostitution) where both adults are consenting, albeit in a way that is shaped by their gender, occupation, ethnicity, socio-economic status and cultural values (Lowman 2000). In-between is a whole host of different locations of exploitation, from casual to full-time, or self-employed to working in pairs or groups. It appears that youth are less often found in off-street work such as escort services or exotic dancing, which are more highly regulated through municipal policies; they primarily work the street or are found in non-regulated off-street work such as gang houses, trick pads, or drug houses. It is argued that by simply being on the street, de-familied and homeless youth find themselves more likely to take part in forms of prostitution (Hoyt, Ryan and Cauce 1999; Whitbeck, Hoyt and Yoder 1999; Weisberg 1985). Other forms of commercial sexual exploitation such as child pornography, child sex rings and the sexual use of minors are beyond the scope of this book.

Partially due to the differing definitions of youth prostitution and partially due to the underground nature of prostitution and street life generally, there are no concrete reliable statistics that reflect the number of youth exploited through prostitution. UNICEF (United Nations Children's Fund) estimates that worldwide one million children a year are sexually exploited. Others estimate the number of children and youth involved in the international sex trade to be between one and ten million (Hedmann et al. 1998; Joseph 1995). Various Canadian studies also report varying estimates. A study in Vancouver estimated that on any given night in 1995 there were thirty to forty youth working on the street (McCarthy 1995). An outreach program in Saskatoon identified ninety-three children under the age of sixteen being exploited on the street in 1996 (Thibodeau 1996). An outreach program in Regina reported that out of 2,700 contacts in 1996, 45 percent or 1,215 were individuals under age eighteen (Street Workers Advocacy Project 1996). A 1994 evaluation of P.O.W.E.R. (Prostitutes and Other Women for Equal Rights) in Winnipeg documented contact with 2,600 different individuals, one third, or 858, of whom were under age eighteen. Police statistics report that from 1986 to 1990, about 10–15 percent of prostitutes arrested under the communicating provision in the *Criminal Code* were in the young offender category (Federal/Provincial/Territorial Working Group Report 1998:16). These numbers have declined, with only 3 percent of 1995 charges of prostitution-related offences involving youth. This most likely reflects the changes in *Criminal Code* and police enforcement practices rather than a decrease in the number of youth working the street.

Who Are They? Age, Gender and Ethnicity

Different reports describe different ages of entry into prostitution. Although age of entry is often difficult to assess given that entry into prostitution is a process, something that occurs over time rather than occurring at a given moment, it is still important to address. The differing reports are important because the variation in numbers reflects different experiences and suggests the use of caution in making sensationalistic generalizations about the age of those involved.

A Victoria survey and British Columbia consultations for the Federal/Provincial/Territorial Working Group on Prostitution (1998) revealed an average entry age of 14 to 15.5 years. A Vancouver study estimated that females entered at age 16.3 and males at an average age of 15.6 years (McCarthy 1995). Benoit and Millar's recent study found age 18 to be the average age of entry (2001). An Ottawa survey found the average age of entry to be 17.8 years (Caputo et al. 1994). The Street Workers Advocacy Project in Regina found that 12 percent of youth on the street were under 12 years old and the average age was reported as between 12 and 14 years old. The National Youth Prostitution Survey in 1987 found that girls became involved at an average age of 14.4 years and males at 15.4 years (Roeters 1987). Shaver (1996) found that most workers began their careers between the ages of 16 and 20.

Research consistently finds that more girls than boys are sexually exploited through prostitution (Badgley 1984; Lowman 1987; Roeters 1987; Shaver 1996; Jiwani 1998). Some Canadian research indicates that the number of male youth exploited through prostitution is growing (Caputo et al. 1994). Shaver reports that males make up 10–25 percent of all street prostitutes (1996). There also exists very different experiences within the male and female sex trades. Generally males appear to be more independent in their work than females, who more often work for a pimp (Campagna and Poffenberger 1988). Men experience work differently and are found to work a more regular schedule and see more clients (Weinberg et al. 1999). Girls tend to exchange sex more often for survival than men do. Males use the street as their primary work site whereas women are scattered, working in brothels, trick pads and escort services (Campagna and Poffenberger 1988). Violent experiences also differ. Male prostitutes are more likely to use violence against customers while female prostitutes are more likely to have violence used against them (Campagna and Poffenberger 1988; Lowman 2000). Males are more likely to be beaten not by their customers, but by others because of their sexual orientation (Campagna and Poffenberger 1988; Shaver 1996). Shaver (1996) also reports that males are less likely to be arrested for prostitution-related offences; this would seem to indicate women are criminalized more often.

Aboriginal youth are overrepresented as youth exploited through prostitution (Miki 1995; First Call 1996; McEvoy and Daniluk 1995, Kingsley and Mark 2000). Due to the location of Aboriginal persons in Canadian society and the history of colonization and cultural genocide, it is argued that Aboriginal women and girls are the most vulnerable to exploitation (Miki 1995; First Call 1996; McEvoy and Daniluk 1995; Brock and Thistlehwaite 1996). Lynne argues that the combination of patriarchy and capitalism has deeply wounded First Nations women, rendering them a sexual commodity:

> Historical patriarchal and capitalist relations subjugated First Nations women collectively. This collective sexual oppression, based on gender, created our inferiority as a class of people to both First Nations men and non–First Nations men. The sexual domination of First Nations women has remained unabated to the present-day due to patriarchy's stronghold. Thus, it has had, and continues to have, profound and prolonged injurious consequences in First Nations women's lives. When sexual oppression is intersected by racism, and capitalism, the wounding worsens—this compounded wounding for First Nations women has occurred for over five hundred years. (1998: 2)

Realities of Work: Substance Use, Pimping, Violence and Stigma

While research on youth prostitution work routines is scant, some work on adult prostitution has included data on youth work.

Most reports indicate a high incidence of substance use and addiction among women in the sex trade (Badgley 1984; Federal/Provincial/Territorial Working Group on Prostitution 1998). Shaver (1996) argues that this might be misleading and substance use varies based on gender and region. She found the highest rates of use in the Atlantic provinces (50 percent of workers were heavy drug users) and the lowest rates in Quebec (16 percent heavy drug users). While it is often argued whether substance use is a precursor to the engagement in prostitution (Brannigan et al. 1989) or a consequence of the work (Fraser 1985; Lowman 1987), it is generally agreed that the relationship between substance use and prostitution is somewhat circular or co-determinate (Schissel and Fedec 1999). Increased abuse of substances often occurs upon entrenchment in street work as a way to cope with the emotional consequences of the work; this results in a continuance of the work as a way to finance increased substance use (Lau 1989; Heinrich 1995).

Pimping is a highly debated topic. Kempadoo and Doezma (1998) discuss prostitution as either forced or voluntary. Many accounts of youth prostitution focus on youth being forced to engage in prostitution and girls as victims of trafficking. However, it is debatable whether pimping is as straightforward as it seems (Lowman 1987). Instead pimping is often a gray area with significant overlaps in how the relationships are defined—pimps versus boyfriends, friends, and girlfriends. Thus, caution should be taken when drawing any conclusions about coercion into prostitution and the role of pimps (Phoenix 1998; O'Neill 2001).

Violence experienced by sex-trade workers is less controversial. Research has consistently found high rates of violence among sex-trade workers (Miller and Schwartz 1995; Dalla 2000; Weinberg et al. 1999). However, little has been done in the area of youth. It is a contentious issue as to whether it is the work of prostitution itself that is hazardous or the way it is currently structured with a lack of health and safety regulation that ultimately places women at risk of experiencing violence (Brock 1998; Shaver 1996; Vanwesenbeeck 2001). Canadian research has questioned whether youth avoidance of policies intended to assist them places them at greater risk to experience violence (Lowman 2000: Bittle 2002).

Recent research indicates that social stigma experienced by adult prostitutes appears to be on the rise. It examines emotional distress of workers experienced as a result of the stigma associated with prostitution. Research among adult workers suggests that women are rarely completely open about their work, which thus places enormous emotional burdens on them (see Ridge, Minichiello and Plummer 1997; Brewis and Linstead 2000).

Why Are They There? Childhood Abuse, Homelessness and Choice

A great deal of research on youth prostitution has focused on reasons for entry into prostitution. Much of the recent work has examined child sexual abuse as a precursor to prostitution and examined issues of homelessness and running away.

It is estimated that a majority of exploited youth have a history of sexual abuse. However, it is unclear whether this history of abuse differs from the history of abuse in the general population. The Badgley Report (1984) found no difference in levels of sexual abuse among youth prostitutes compared to the population at large. Brannigan, Kanfla and Levy (1989) found the same in a Calgary study. Others, however, found that childhood sexual abuse is a major factor contributing to becoming involved with, and vulnerable to, later sexual exploitation through prostitution. A Montreal study of prostitutes found that 45 percent had been victims of incest before becoming prostitutes (Gemme et al. 1984). Bagley and Young (1987) found similarly high levels of abuse reported.

Given these disagreements there is much debate about whether child sexual abuse is a precursor to prostitution. This may in fact be a non-issue. While it appears these women generally have a higher-than-average experience of sexual abuse, there is also evidence that this should not be regarded as a causal relationship (Mathews 1989; Brannigan and Van Brunschot 1997). Rather, it appears that the intersection of family situation and abusive experiences within the family, culminating with running away; a lack of viable alternatives for youth generally; and a failure of the child welfare system create the situation where prostitution occurs (Chesney-Lind and Shelden 1992; Schissel and Fedec 1999).

Most research indicates that youth end up on the street for two reasons: an unstable home life and a failure of the child welfare system to assist them (Mathews 1989). Thus, there appears to be a general pattern. A youth will leave home because of dysfunction that may include physical and/or sexual violence perpetrated against her/him by a family member, witnessing domestic violence, general neglect, and/or drug abuse. The youth will generally have contact with some helping agency, most likely a provincially mandated agency. The majority of youth don't find success with programs like these and end up as runaways from group homes who find themselves homeless on the street. As they become entrenched in street life, they increasingly become vulnerable to exploitation through prostitution. Encouraged by friends and street peers, tired and hungry youth engage in selling sex by choice—a choice that is fuelled by necessity. Many engage in the sex trade as the only viable means of survival and feel empowered by being self-sufficient.

Canadian research consistently found that youth prostitutes were either uninformed about accessing social assistance, ineligible for assistance because of their transient lifestyle and age, or simply not prepared to subsist on welfare-level incomes or low skill jobs. Indeed, Vanwesenbeeck, in a review of sex-trade research over the past ten years, found that the most common and obvious factor for entry into prostitution was economic need (2001: 262). Phoenix argues that while adults usually cite inadequate benefits or income as one reason for their entrance into prostitution, for young people "inadequate" usually means nonexistent: entrance into the legitimate labour force and the provision of social security benefits are age restricted (2002: 361-362). Sullivan (1988) indicates there are significant economic incentives for youth to prostitute. However, the amount of money to be made on the street is debated. While the Badgley report indicated that female youth can make up to $40,000 a year working the street: when compared with the average annual income for women ($9,522), it is easy to see the economic gain to be made. However, other research argues that the amount of money is not great and is indeed a misconception of sex-trade work generally (Shaver 1996; Lowman 1998).

Much of the resistance to assisting those involved in prostitution comes from the commonly held notion that people freely choose to engage in prostitution. Thus, since it is an individual choice, any negative experiences are regarded as consequences of a personal choice and the responsibility of the individuals themselves. A study from Save The Children Canada, *Canadian Attitudes about Children in the Sex Trade,* found that 47 percent of those surveyed agreed that most young sex trade workers actually "chose to do it" (Bruton 2000). Others refute this notion of free choice, indicating that choice is constantly mediated by factors outside our control. Lowman argues:

> Once we transcend a phenomenal level of analysis to consider the context of a youth's choice to sell sexual services, it becomes obvious that the choice must be located in the "wider origins of the deviant act," particularly the marginal position of youth in the labour force, and patriarchal power structures both inside and outside the family. (1987: 111)

It is clear that some segments of the population are more vulnerable to having to make this choice than are others. Jiwani (1998), in theorizing about global commercial exploitation, expands reasons for vulnerability to include larger socio-structural contributors such as poverty, marginalization, devaluation of women and girls, previous experiences of violence, racism, and the intersection of these issues with one another. Indeed she argues that some individuals such as gay and lesbian youth, Aboriginal and migrant/immigrant girls, and the poor are in positions where they are more vulnerable to choosing sex-trade work simply because of these characteristics. Homophobia, racism and cultural genocide, and lack of opportunities for the poor impact on children's decisions to run away and seek approval from other sources.

Larger socio-economic issues creating the situation for prostitution to exist need to be examined. The context of sexuality, the sexualization of female bodies and the inequitable attitudes about male and female social roles (paired with the cultural conception and exploitative sexualization of youth and sex) contribute to the situation where prostitution can occur, while also determining who is most vulnerable. This wider social construction of youth and sexuality also plays a role in creating the demand for young female prostitutes, increasing opportunities for their participation. As Mathews (1989) indicates, analysis of youth prostitution must include issues such as unfair differences in male/female socialization (rendering women as submissive and men as dominant), the disenfranchisement of youth from institutional decision making and labour market employment, the failure of social services to assist street youth (indicated in the high number of homeless youth), and the lack of political will to enable families to provide quality care for their children. Thus, we must ask how the decision to prostitute intersects with the power and economic inequities between males and females, and between adults and children. A lack of adequate job opportunities and housing for youth combines with the sexual demand for young women to make prostitution appear as a viable source of income and independence.

The Girl Child Project[2]

This volume aims to advance our understanding of the experiences of girls exploited through prostitution and ways to best respond to the issue. Each chapter describes a distinct component of a research project that was conducted by the tri-provincial research network RESOLVE (Research and Education for Solutions to Violence and Abuse).[3] Following a preliminary year of funding by Status of Women Canada to undertake research on violence prevention and the girl child, RESOLVE focused three subsequent years of research on the issue of sexual exploitation through prostitution.

The focus of this work was to examine the lives, and to hear the voices, of girls sexually exploited through prostitution. Although there is considerable research on prostitution generally, there is a paucity of research on girls and adolescents who are sexually exploited through prostitution and a lack of research that allows youth to explain their own perceptions of their needs. This research asked girls to describe their experiences with programming (how it helped or harmed them) and to identify service gaps and best practices. In addition to issues of programming, the girls were given the opportunity to speak about their experience of identity formation, social networks, health issues, experiences of violence and the factors that push them into and may draw them out of prostitution.

The research applied three main methods. First was an examination of service provision in Canada. A total of 173 agencies were canvassed[4] in a program review of each Canadian province on existing policies and programs for sexually exploited and street youth. Of these agencies, innovative programs were selected for site visits and in-depth service provider interviews. Forty-three interviews were conducted. Second, we interviewed fifty-four adult women and men who had become involved in prostitution before age eighteen. These interviews took place in Manitoba, Saskatchewan and Alberta. And finally, we undertook an examination of the legal issues related to the topic. This examination assessed new legislation and the capacity of the current child welfare acts across the country to accommodate intervention strategies for this group of youth.

The interviews with women and men were done using a semi-structured interview schedule. The only requirement for taking part in the interviews was that the participants had been involved in sex-trade work as youth. The participants told their stories in their own way and thus not every respondent discussed the same issues. Further, each of the three RESOLVE teams in the three Prairie provinces had a somewhat different emphasis and this is reflected in some of the interview outcomes. With the exception of four focus groups ranging from two to four participants, the interviews were conducted individually. The participants were recruited through their past or current involvement with specialized services for prostitution, counselling, criminal diversion programs or substance abuse.

Several limitations are worth noting. As previously mentioned, interviews were conducted differently in the three provinces, allowing for tailoring to the special interests of the research team members. This means that not all respondents were asked similar questions. The women respondents were contacted because of their involvement with agencies; therefore, we only spoke with those who had perceived a need to be involved with formal services. This group may be different from others working in prostitution who have chosen not to seek help or it may be more reflective of street prostitution than of other forms such as working in escort services. Further, the demographics of those interviewed varied greatly across the three provinces. Alberta respondents were mostly Caucasian and were younger, in contrast to interviewees from Saskatchewan and Manitoba, where a high proportion were of First Nations background, and many were older. We cannot ascertain whether this reflects actual differences in who becomes involved in prostitution in the three provinces or is an artifact of the way that we obtained participants.

In reading this volume, three things must be taken into account. First, the participants often had a difficult time distinguishing between life on the street as youth and as adults. Although we do our best to separate the experiences, the continuity of experience becomes diminished when we do so. Thus, more often than not, the experiences revealed here are both those that occurred to participants as youth and as young adults. Second, although we interviewed men, we have included only women in the analyses presented here. The number of men we interviewed was quite small and so they were excluded from these analyses. Also, we interviewed some women who were eighteen and over when they began sex-trade work. In the effort to focus on youth experience, these women's narratives were excluded. Therefore, throughout the volume, the number of narratives analyzed in each chapter varies between forty-five and forty-seven due to individual researcher categories. Also, the terminology used to refer to the participants is women and often "the women." The third and most important issue is around terminology. The terminology surrounding youth engagement in the sex trade is a difficult one. The difficulty stems from how one conceptualizes youth prostitutes: solely as victims, as agents, or as a combination of both. This difficulty was reflected within our research team. While some preferred the term sex trade, others found it unacceptable in that it didn't capture the abusive and exploitive nature of prostitution; others found the term exploitation or exploited youth to be too victimizing. Therefore throughout this volume various terms will be used, such as youth/girls/women exploited through prostitution, prostituted youth/girls/women, youth/girls/women involved in the sex trade or sex-trade work, youth/girls/women involved in prostitution, and youth prostitutes.

Demographics and Background of the Women

As mentioned, the analyses in this volume are based on 45 interviews with women from Alberta, Saskatchewan and Manitoba who had been involved in prostitution before age eighteen.[5] Of these women, a higher percentage were of Aboriginal descent (26 or 57.7 percent) than Caucasian (19 or 42.2 percent). This proportion was different across the three provinces, with the Saskatchewan interviews exclusively Aboriginal, Manitoba 70 percent Aboriginal, but Alberta only 22.2 percent.

At the time of the interviews, the women ranged in age from 18 to 36: 10 (22.2 percent) were 20 or below, 14 (31.1 percent) were aged between 21 and 25, 11 (24.4 percent) were between 26 and 30, and 9 (20 percent) were 30 or older (one respondent did not specify age). With respect to the age at which they became involved with prostitution, 17 women (37.8 percent) were between 11 and 13; 16 (35.6 percent) became involved between 14 and 15, and 12 (26.7 percent) were aged 16 to 17. Thus, almost three quarters of the women began their involvement when they were 15 years old or less.

Almost 40 percent of the women had been involved for five years or less, another third (34.7 percent) for over eleven years, and 22.2 percent had six to ten years of involvement. The participants were almost equally divided between those who had left the streets (51 percent) and those who were still involved (49 percent). As children, 63 percent of the respondents had been involved with the child welfare system. Of these, most (77.8 percent) had been taken into care and resided in foster and group homes, often for many years. A high proportion (32 or 71 percent) of the respondents reported an abuse history as children. Of those who reported abuse, 21 (65.6 percent) had been sexually abused, most by family members. Only five individuals noted that they had not been abused in their families. Thirteen respondents did not mention that they had been abused as children, although a number of these had been taken into care by child welfare authorities, indicating significant problems in their families of origin.

Fifteen women became pregnant while under the age of eighteen and while they were on the streets; they bore one or more children. Of these, nine no longer have custody, although some visit their children, who live with relatives.

Hearing the Voices of the Women

This volume speaks to current debates and concerns of sex trade research outlined above, often questioning common assumptions and public notions of life on the street. This is done through hearing the voices of sex-trade involved women.

The book begins with "Selling Sex? It's Really Like Selling Your Soul": Vulnerability to and the Experience of Exploitation through Child Prostitution." Leslie Tutty and Kendra Nixon examine the push and pull factors for young women on the street. They examine the issue of childhood sexual, emotional and physical abuse as a precursor to life on the street. Further, they examine the avoidance of state-mandated services and homelessness as reasons for sex-trade work. They also discuss the definition of prostitution as survival sex and engage in the debate on economic incentive. Money is discussed as an important factor in keeping women on the street, but is also viewed in terms of its addiction and fluidity. The chapter also sheds light on issues of pimping and begins to question the traditional conception of pimps in the lives of young women, finding that many women do not distinguish between pimp and boyfriend. Questioning the common notion of forced prostitution by males, the chapter examines the finding that many girls learned the ropes from other girls rather than being pimped by men. The chapter also discusses transitioning from the street and the stigma that many women with few outside choices endure in the face of poverty.

Stigma is a central issue on how women internalize their experiences and craft their identities as prostitutes and as women. In "The People We Think We Are," Pamela Downe examines how young women in prostitution create self-identities. Age, drugs (as a way to cope with stigma), emotions (such as anger and fear), family, friends, gender, cultural location, race, parenthood, self-esteem and sexuality are examined within the broader analysis of how women intimately affected by prostitution come to view themselves in relation to the world around them. This chapter sets out the ways in which the women have internalized their experiences as former youth prostitutes in Canada and how that continues to affect them currently.

Detailed accounts of violence experienced in families of origin, on the street as sex workers, and by societal institutions are examined in the third chapter, "That Was My Prayer Every Night—Just To Get Home Safe." Kendra Nixon and Leslie Tutty present a convincing case that girls involved in prostitution are a highly victimized population. This chapter examines the experience of violence as related in many ways to the stigma attached to the work (violence by the general public) and how the stigma is internalized by young women through forms of self-harm (such as suicide attempts, self-mutilation). It also documents resiliency and management of risk associated with street work such as survival and safety strategies.

In Chapter Four, "I Don't Know What the Hell It Is But It Sounds Nasty," the health and well-being of women and girls in the sex trade is of paramount concern. Little is known about how these young women actually experience, assess, prioritize and respond to health-threatening conditions. The women discuss how experiences with, as well as knowledge and fear of, HIV/AIDS, Hepatitis-C, addictions, fatigue, mental illness and trauma are recounted in their life on the streets. Bio-medical models are questioned as the appropriate way in which to frame health concerns of sex-trade workers. A discussion of how the women have utilized the health care resources as well as the prevailing use and abuse of prescription medication also figures prominently in this chapter.

Chapter Five reviews the Canadian structure of child welfare legislation including traditional child welfare intervention models, as well as the newer protective confinement regimes in place in Alberta and British Columbia. Karen Busby argues that such regimes deny rights guaranteed by the *Charter of Rights and Freedoms* and questions how these denials are justified by governments. She explores the issue of gender as it relates to confinement models and state intervention.

Providing services to youth involved in the sex trade is explored by Kelly Gorkoff and Meghan Waters under the umbrella statement of "Balancing Safety, Respect and Choice in Programs for Young Women Involved in Prostitution." This chapter reviews three primary modes of service delivery for youth in the sex trade: state-mandated service, special legislative initiatives and non-governmental programs. The chapter contrasts the lived experiences of youth and compassion of service providers within the three models. It addresses debates among service providers and among youth on the most effective service delivery as well as the differing experiences with apprehension models. It concludes with some policy concerns distinct to Canada and demands that larger social concerns be brought to bear on programming issues.

Overall, the collection of chapters contained in this volume gives voice to a population whose voices need to be heard. Through examining the various issues presented in this volume, we can begin to appreciate the complexities of the lives of young women exploited through prostitution. As the women courageously share their stories, you will hear their pain, their struggles and their fears, and you will know that childhoods have been lost. Their voices will challenge your own thoughts and beliefs of this issue and take you to a higher level of understanding the realities of this life. Is this a lifestyle choice? No. Is this an easy way to make money? No. Each chapter clearly describes the harsh realities of sexual exploitation, how it affects these women's relationships, health, esteem and identity and how this turns into a vicious cycle that becomes difficult to escape.

The answers to this issue are here, as long as these women's voices are "Being Heard."

Notes

1. See work by advocate groups such as COYOTE (Call off your tired old ethics), Maggies, Stella, SWAV (Sex Workers Advocacy Project of Vancouver), website <www.walnet.org>. It is interesting to note however, that while these groups advocate for health, safety and choice among adults involved in sex-trade work, youth are sometimes left out of their approach: the argument is focused on consenting adults, and advocating is for those over age eighteen.

2. This description of the research, its limitations, and demographics is a version of "Examination of Innovative Prgramming for Children and Youth

Involved in Prostitution" by Busby, Downe, Gorkoff, Nixon, Tutty and Ursel, in Berman and Jiwani 2002, pages 89–113. For that report the majority of what is included here was compiled and written by Leslie Tutty.

3. RESOLVE is one of five Centres of Excellence across Canada originally funded in 1992 by the Family Violence Initiative to study Violence against Women and Children. This project was conducted as part of a larger study of the Alliance of Five Research Centres on Violence. A condensed version of all of the chapters in this volume can be found in Berman and Jiwani 2002.

4. Working east to west, we conducted 18 interviews in the Atlantic provinces, 17 in Quebec, 69 in Ontario, 8 in Manitoba, 11 in Saskatchewan, 24 in Alberta, and 26 in British Columbia.

5. This includes one transgendered person.

Chapter One

"Selling Sex?
It's Really Like Selling Your Soul"
Vulnerability to and the Experience of
Exploitation through Child Prostitution

Leslie Tutty and Kendra Nixon

How do girls and adolescents under age eighteen become involved in prostitution? What were their lives like beforehand and what keeps them from exiting back to mainstream society? Is substance misuse a point of entry or does it develop into the rationale for continuing exploitation? In what ways are youth sexually exploited? How many are controlled by pimps or trafficked internationally? What proportion of adolescents sexually exploited through prostitution exit before they are adults and how do they accomplish this? This chapter explores these questions based on the narratives of forty-seven women from Canada's three Prairie provinces. It examines the factors that left them vulnerable to being exploited as girls or adolescents, their circumstances while on the streets and their attempts to leave. In each section, where available, we provide an overview of the findings of other researchers that focus on the same issues.

Of children and young women exploited through prostitution in Canada, a high proportion is of Aboriginal origin, even in centres in which the population of individuals of Aboriginal background is relatively small (Kingsley and Mark 2000). Thus, in the qualitative analysis of our interviews, we compared the themes identified by the twenty-six Aboriginal women to those of the twenty Caucasian women (an additional African Canadian woman was not included in this comparison). In most instances the issues were indistinguishable; however, we highlight those that differentiated Aboriginal from Caucasian women since these might be important in developing strategies to prevent exploitation or to assist involved women.

Background and Context Before Entry Into Prostitution

Researchers have identified several factors associated with a vulnerability to sexual exploitation through prostitution. A high proportion of these girls and young women were sexually abused as children (McIntyre 1999; Schissel and Fedec 1999) and many were taken into care by the child welfare system, living in group homes or foster homes (Estes 2001; Kingsley and Mark 2000).

The women that we interviewed reported similarly high levels of child sexual abuse. Of the thirty-three who commented about any childhood abuse, 91 percent had been victimized sexually, several by a number of offenders. The most common perpetrators were fathers, stepfathers, or other male adults including their mothers' boyfriends.

Not only did the premature, unwanted and abusive introduction to sexual activity set a pattern for perceiving sex between adults and children as essentially "normal," one father and one stepfather paid or tried to pay their daughters for sex. As one commented, "I was paid to do it by my dad. That's how the chain works. One person ... pays you and then you just get started. [Then you ran away and started doing it on the street?] Yes." The other woman described, "My stepfather, before I prostituted, tried to offer me two hundred dollars to sleep with him and then twisted it around when I went to my mom, and said 'she tried to get it from me.' My mother believed him.... I tried to shoot him because what he was saying was not true."

A large number of children run to the streets from either their homes or child welfare placements (Mathews 1989; Badgley 1984). However, not all sexually exploited youth come from child welfare backgrounds. Others, called "throwaway" children, are from families that no longer want them or can no longer handle them (National Centre for Missing and Exploited Children 1998). Slightly less than two-thirds of the women with whom we talked had been involved with the child welfare system before being sexually exploited through prostitution. Of these, most had been taken into care and resided in foster and group homes, often for a number of years.

> Started working downtown when I was twelve to thirteen years old. I was taken from my mom when I was three; in seven different foster homes; adopted when I was five. There I was sexually abused by numerous cousins and my brother. I left home when I was twelve.

> [Were you in foster homes?] Yes, and I ran. They weren't my parents; I didn't have to listen to them. Child welfare never offered me any counselling, never talked to me, just moved me, moved me, and moved me. I've been in institutions and that's when I started.

While thirteen women did not mention having been abused as children, a number had been taken into care by child welfare authorities, indicating significant problems in their families of origin. Several other women, however, made a point of noting that they came from what they considered "normal" families. As one woman who started prostituting at age twelve mentioned, "I lived at home with my parents. I've always had a good relationship with my parents." Another, who had similarly become involved when twelve years old, commented, "I came from a normal family in a small town in Alberta. Both my parents worked. They weren't abusive in any way." Ironically, she later described her parents as yelling, locking the door on her and calling her names.

The extent to which the girls had been sexually abused and were living away from their families of origin immediately before becoming involved in prostitution is notable and is similar to the experiences of others exploited by prostitution as children (see McIntyre 1999; Estes 2001)

Introduction Into Sexual Exploitation

The women described the ways in which they became enticed or coerced into prostitution. Virtually all, as girls, had someone who provided them information about how to "turn tricks" and who normalized prostitution, presenting it as a viable option.

Estes (2001) previously described adolescents who became exploited through prostitution because they have friends or family members already involved. These familiar adolescents or adults either normalize the behaviour indirectly through role modelling or directly encourage youth to become involved. Some of the women that we interviewed similarly lived in environments in which prostitution was common. Ten had family members involved in prostitution: five had sisters, four had mothers (one of these also had a grandmother) involved. Two had fathers who were pimps; one father not only pimped his daughter but his wife as well.

> I grew up literally on the street because my mom was a prostitute and I was brought up in that environment. We used to live in those hotels and I used to watch the hookers from the rooftop. Like my babysitter was, I think, a hooker. It just ran in the family. (Started at fifteen)

> My sisters were doing it at the time. I was living with my mom and I learned from them. And then I started seeing some of their regulars. I was used to being around them and I don't know, just started. It was good money. (Started at age fourteen)

> My older sister worked too, so that's how I got into it ... my sister did a lot of talking ... I saw the money and the things she had. (Started at age thirteen)

The typical public perception of how those exploited through prostitution enter the sex trade is that girls get enticed and recruited by male pimps. This is often not the case. Rather, girls may become involved through female peers who suggest this alternative—an independent means to survive (Tyler, Hoyt, Whitbeck and Cauce 2001; Raychaba 1993). Twice as many of the women that we interviewed had "learned the ropes" from other girls their own age, as had been pimped by young men.

> I was fifteen. I had been ripped away from my family and shoved in a group home. I took off, met a girl and I spotted for her—watching the cars and I learned everything about it.

> I started when I was about eighteen right after my sister died. She was murdered—beaten to death. My sister used to do it, once in awhile. She never taught me or told me to do it. We lived on the drag and I was just watching the girls and I met a girl who told me what to do.

> My friends were all doing it. I figured, "I can too." So I started selling myself. I learned about sex, how to hustle, how to stand. Just picking it up from other people. (Started at sixteen)

About one-quarter of the women were groomed by pimps or by "boyfriends" who encouraged them to become involved in prostitution. One woman who started at age fourteen described how she "met a pimp at [a local bar]. Because I was running away and had no money it was really easy for him to get me out there—that was about it. A second women narrated, "I was sixteen, I had just left home. I had nowhere to go and [another woman] said she could hook me up with a guy who'd get me onto the street and look after me. I didn't have any other choice." For a third woman who started at age eleven, the process did not have an obvious beginning:

> I was just a kid. I didn't know nothing. So, here was this nice guy who was twenty-five and like this older brother. At first nothin' was going on. Then he started getting off on me bit by bit. Then he started bringin' his friends over, to try me out. The next thing, I'm workin' at his parties. I was too dumb to even know that he was makin' money off me.

Four women, however, were coerced into prostitution:

> I was fourteen. I had run into some people I thought were friends and ended

up being put on the street. I was drugged up, then I was put out. [Were you threatened?] Yep.

I was thirteen. I had a gun held to my head.

I was fifteen. This woman ... her brother took me to Saskatoon. We were drinking and the next morning she said, 'If she's going to stay here, she's going to have to work.' Next thing I know they're putting dresses on me (I was a tomboy). They did my makeup and my hair. Dropped me off downtown and told me, next car that pulled up I had to get in.

Several women chose to enter into prostitution. One, who started at age fifteen, commented, "I just went out on the street and did it. Me and my best friend. That's how I lost my virginity." Another woman mentioned that at age sixteen, "I was low on money and wanted some drugs or whatever, so me and my girlfriend decided that we would just go for a walk—we wouldn't stand on the corner or anything—but we would just go for a little walk and, if something happened ... and it did."

Stated Reasons for the First Experience in Prostitution

In addition to the description of incidents that the women identified as precipitating their first exploitation through prostitution, we were interested in broader factors that led to the streets. Needing money for basic needs and for drugs has been associated with such sexual exploitation. Children on the streets often engage in what is termed "survival sex," to pay for food, shelter and other necessities. Survival sex is the sale of sexual services by those such as homeless youth and women in poverty who have few other options. With few legitimate means of support, youth may resort to survival sex or are coerced into prostitution (Silbert and Pines 1981; Weisberg 1985). Some also engage in petty crime, such as theft, robbery and conning, to survive (Hagan and McCarthy 1997; Whitbeck, Hoyt and Yoder 1999).

Kingsley and Mark identified three stages in becoming involved in the sex trade. First is the process of "drift" from abuse and/or casual sex to the first act of prostitution. Second is alternating between soliciting and a more conventional life. For those who remain, the next stage is that of becoming "professional," where "one associates entirely with others in the sex trade, where they find themselves accepted for who and what they are" (Kingsley and Mark 2000: 33). The others become their "street family," assisting and supporting them and often teaching them how to engage in prostitution to meet basic needs (Estes 2001; McIntyre 1999). The end result is a feeling of belonging and community that fills the emotional gaps created in a childhood of abuse and abandonment, but this also makes it difficult to exit.

Above, the women described the "how" of their first incident of prostituting. But what were the immediate circumstances that resulted in this "decision"—the "why?" Money was a key factor in becoming involved for the women with whom we spoke, but for different reasons. The three most commonly mentioned reasons for needing money were for survival (food and shelter), for drugs and alcohol and for the pursuit of what some thought would be a glamorous lifestyle.

Acquiring money for drugs, either for themselves or their boyfriends (fifteen women), was the most frequently cited motivation:

> I was quite popular, really good in school. It wasn't until I started getting involved with drugs and alcohol that I started having problems. A month or two into grade eight, I dropped out. If I would have [had] that awareness of drugs and alcohol problems … unfortunately I became a victim of it. That's how I explain it. (Started at fourteen)

> We used a lot of drugs, crack cocaine. When he [boyfriend] wanted money, I tried everything to get the money by legal means, but being fourteen years old, you don't have a whole lot of options. I put him off for at least four or five days. He said, "why don't you do this?" It was intended to be one night only: one night turned into two. (Started at fourteen)

> I met someone who told me he loved me. I fell into his game and he addicted me to crack cocaine and put me out on the street to pay for my habit later on. (Started at thirteen)

Acquiring money for drugs needs to be understood in the context of the broader life circumstances in which the young women lived. Most commented about needing substances without elaborating on the poverty, family abandonment and lack of shelter that led to their current drug use and their existence on the streets. Yet these experiences were clearly central to finding themselves on this pathway.

The second most common reason, mentioned by twelve women, all of whom had run away from home or foster care as girls, was to meet basic needs such as food and shelter, that is, they engaged in what is called "survival sex" (Hoyt et al. 1999; Janus et al. 1987; Whitbeck et al. 1999). Three times as many Caucasian women noted this, compared to women of Aboriginal origin. The reasons for this are not clear: it may be that the Aboriginal women were more likely to have always experienced chronic poverty or to have family or friends already involved in prostitution, whereas a higher proportion of the Caucasian girls had run away from home and then found themselves destitute. One young woman who was thirteen described, "I had nowhere to go, no money, no food, nobody to take care of me." Another narrated:

> We were the mall rats living in the basement. There were thirteen of us—everybody else was younger. I was fifteen or sixteen. It was really hard to keep them fed, so that's when I started working. There was always a lot of alcohol and drugs around, but never money for food. There was a little girl—somebody offered her money to see her breasts. She was thirteen. I did it instead. We had one girl who was twelve and she hadn't eaten for four days. Another little girl who was nine and the same. After that, I just kind of did it all the time.

In contrast, ten adolescents, all of whom still lived at home, were lured by the promise of money, and, for some, the "glamour" of the lifestyle. The majority of these were of Aboriginal background. Although they didn't elaborate on their family circumstances, a number lived near the strolls/track/street (a specific area, usually a few city blocks, where sex trade people work), typically in the poorer sections of the city.

> It was the thing to do. When you're thirteen years old, you need bucks bad. They say to young girls—you can have this, you can have that. [It seemed glamorous?] Yes.

> I thought money—cool. I want to be like that. I saw these girls wearing fur coats and I thought they were cool. They had this, they had that, you know, dope, whatever—always had cigarettes, always had money to drink—stuff like that.

> Other girls who worked told me to meet these guys and they put me on the streets. I was thirteen. [Were they pimps?] Not really. Just wanna-bes. I was impressed by the clothes, the lifestyle that I thought they were leading. The money. Drinking. Drugs. Partying.

Exploited on the Streets, Exploited Elsewhere

Just as there are different life circumstances that lead to sexual exploitation, the involvement itself takes a number of forms. As discussed in the introduction to this book, sexual exploitation occupies a continuum incorporating forms of street work, escort service work, brothels and massage parlours. According to authors such as Miller (1993), street prostitution is the most misunderstood and mythologized occupation. Kingsley and Marks (2000) estimated that only 5 to 20 percent of commercial sexual exploitation is visible on the streets, so focusing on street prostitution addresses only a small proportion of those affected by sexual exploitation. They also noted that in smaller communities, prostitution is often hidden, with youth exchanging sex for food and shelter, rather than for money, in such a way that this activity may not be perceived as sexual exploitation. This pattern likely exists in urban centres as well.

After initial experiences with sexual exploitation, what does life hold for women who continue prostituting? Most of the women with whom we spoke were heavily involved in street prostitution as adolescents, working almost every day. Almost half had been involved for five years or less, a quarter had six to ten years of involvement, and a third over eleven years. Several described a typical day:

> I'd be in bed until about two in the afternoon, get up, and I'd still live a half decent normal life during the day. I'd go shopping and this and that. About seven or eight—once it got dark—I'd go down to the stroll and work until three in the morning after bar rush, go to an after-hours club, stay out until six in the morning, go home, start again. That's the cycle.

> Sleep during the day and wake up, get ready, eat, probably go out about eight or nine, work all night—usually work, score, work, score, work, score—like dope—and then be done about seven in the morning, and then sleep all day and wake up at five, get ready, go out at eight or nine. Work all night. It was like that for years.

> I used to treat it as a job. I'd go to work at noon or one and every day in summer, I worked until four in the morning.

> I basically stood out there in a short mini skirt, in the middle of winter, of course, freezing my butt off. All I had to do at the time was blows and hand jobs because I was thirteen. I started doing lays when I was fifteen, fourteen and a half. I always used a condom though.

Although these women worked primarily on the street, a number had experienced different forms of exploitation. Eleven women travelled or were trafficked across the country or the continent as adolescents, prostituting in various cities.

> It was a lot different when I was fourteen, fifteen because of the people and the "family" that I was with. They were from the States where I spent most of my time. This circuit's a lot more violent, a lot more controlling. At any given time, someone—my pimp or his brother or cousin—could drive by or be across the street or in the pool hall down the road.

> I was mainly in it when I was about sixteen to eighteen. That's when I was—a "ho'" [street language for whore]. I was proud of the fact I was a prostitute. I went to Montreal for six months—I'd come back. I went to Vancouver for a

couple of weeks. I went to Calgary for a bit and I came back. I went to Edmonton. I was working. It was a matter of just going where the money was.

I was back and forth from Edmonton and here. I hitchhiked to Toronto when I was thirteen. Went out there and worked on the streets and then all pimps tried to come after me so I came back here and.... [Coming after you—to work for them?] Yeah. They were pretty intimidating. Toronto is a pretty crazy city for a little thirteen-year-old girl to be in.

Three women worked for escort services as teens, even though, as one commented, this was illegal.

[You worked from thirteen?] Yeah. I've worked massage parlours, escort agencies. I've never danced. I've been offered to dance before I had my children.

I was part of an escort agency, just before I was fifteen, for about two months. We were supposed to be eighteen years old to work there but we were fourteen, fifteen. There were three girlfriends of mine. That was probably the only time that I would say I was pimped.

Pimps

Just as pimps did not introduce the majority of women to the streets, most women managed their own activities for a considerable portion of their time on the street. Nine women had never been involved with a pimp. As several of these women stated:

I had heard too many bad things about pimps. They are supposed to be protection. It's not like I didn't know any pimps. What's the point—these guys don't even have a car. What are they going to do? If you get beat up are they going to catch the next bus and come and get you? I didn't want to be forced. If I went out, it was on my own time, when I wanted to do it. I didn't want to give my money to anybody. I did it for my own profit.

I've worked for about eight years and I've never had a pimp. So it was more voluntary and it was completely for drugs.

Nevertheless, a number were involved with pimps for at least one period on the street, many against their wishes.

The first year I was being pimped. I was told to go out and get so much money and stay where I was supposed to. They were always watching me.

I was pimped till I was eighteen and then I argued against the fact that men were keeping my money and I'd be sold off all of a sudden. I'd walk into the bar, go to cash in and then I was told to go to Regina or, "by the way you're going to Edmonton." By the time I was eighteen, nineteen, I decided "piss on you all" and I worked for myself. Independently.

It was sometimes difficult to distinguish pimps from intimate partners or boyfriends who also expected the girls to bring in money by prostituting themselves. Not uncommonly, the relationship began as girlfriend/boyfriend and then the man began requesting that she prostitute for money to purchase shelter or drugs.

> I really loved him. I thought, "I'll work the street for this guy." We're doing drugs and life was perfect. I wanted to spend the rest of my life with him, hooking and doing drugs. To me, that was utopia. But it was short-lived. I only hooked for two months and got arrested.

> I think he was just happy that he had some girls making money for him. As long as he had money in his pocket he was happy. [Did you have sex with him as well?] Yeah. [Kind of a boyfriend slash pimp?]. Right. [Which they all are?] Yeah.

> I used to have an old man. Like he needed smokes or he needed to eat or whatever, he'd send me out. And sometimes I'd go out there and I didn't want to be out there.

One difference between pimps and boyfriends was that pimps tended to have more than one girl, compared to boyfriends.

> At that time, the girl I was staying with, we had a man, the same man. It wasn't long before she left too and then it was just me, and he had somebody else. We lived in a hotel.

> One time I was with this guy who had five girls and we were like a family. [Another woman] was older.... I guess we thought she was pretty old, I think she was twenty. But we were all anywhere from about fifteen to eighteen, you know, so she was the old ho'—sort of like our mentor in a sick sort of way.

Several women spoke of recent changes in the way in which street prostitution is organized. They mentioned that gangs have become involved and there are increasing numbers of very young girls on the street buying addictive drugs:

> The gangs are out now pimping the girls. They kidnapped one girl, took her to [a small town] and raped her. They had her for a week and finally she got away. I used to like gangs because they were fighting for their rights. But then later you realize what they're into.

> There are women out there undercutting [charging less than the going rate]. They're young. It ruins us. Most of them are just doing it for a fast rock [crack] or a fast shot in the arm. So when we go out the guy says, "Oh well, I can get a girl for ten, fifteen dollars."

Before it used to be a street family, but now you can't even trust your own best friend out there. It's just going nuts. That's why I don't like hanging out with people. Sometimes I just do my business and go home. To heck with the socializing, it's too dangerous out there.

Drug Use

As noted throughout this book, those involved in prostitution commonly use alcohol and other addictive substances (Dalla 2002; Federal/Provincial/Territorial Working Group on Prostitution 1998). Whether or not this is viewed as preceding entry into prostitution (Brannigan and Fleischman 1989) or as a consequence of such involvement (Fraser 1985; Lowman 1987) has been debated. If nothing else, addiction to substances becomes a factor that interferes with leaving the streets (McIntyre 1999).

Although drug use was a constant in the lives of the women with whom we spoke, most had not used hard (injected) drugs before they were on the streets. Some used substances to numb their fears while they worked; others worked straight so that they could protect themselves in the event of danger. As adolescents, fourteen women, mostly of Caucasian background, used non-injected drugs such as marijuana, acid and prescription pills when on the streets, although alcohol use was common. One woman commented, "I was doing pot—that's all I ever did. I would do, and if I wanted to quit, I would quit and that's all there was. So I was never addicted to anything really bad." Another stated, "I drank wine to try to make me feel like I wasn't part of the seedy street." A third noted, "I just smoked pot and drank vodka and I never got into cocaine until I was about eighteen."

Over half the women routinely used drugs such as cocaine, solvents, crack and heroin, or used needles on a regular basis. Of these, almost twice as many were of Aboriginal background.

I've been addicted to drugs since I was fifteen. I did cocaine. After eighteen months, I started sniffing coke, cocaine, with friends, at bars. It gradually progressed to smoking [crack].

I was fourteen [when I started]. I've worked for about eight years and it was completely for drugs. I didn't start heroin until five years ago, but before that it (prostituting) wasn't every night, it was every second night or when I needed the money. When I was on junk, I'd get so sick without it that I'd have to be working. I'd have to have money for drugs to be OK.

I was into the dope really bad because by the time I was like seventeen, I started fixing. And so of course I was supporting my drug habit and supporting my children.

Becoming Mothers

Perhaps nothing highlights the dilemmas faced by young adolescents sexually exploited through prostitution as much as their narratives about becoming pregnant and what happened to their children because they were identified as prostitutes. As mentioned elsewhere in the book (see Introduction and Chapter Two), fifteen women had become pregnant while under age eighteen and bore one or more children while they were on the streets. Of these, nine no longer have custody, although several continue to visit children who live with relatives.

> I quit a few times when I was carrying my first. I had my daughter, had her taken away by child welfare. [And placed her with your grandma?] Yes.

> I live two different lives. I'm a mother, and I'm a daughter and I'm a working person. I have no children in my care. This is my eighth pregnancy, seventh live birth. [Where are your kids now?] They live with their grandmother.

> I knew I'd have my child taken away if I didn't quit. I remember thinking that I'd have to physically remove myself in order to keep the child. [Get away from the temptation of the street?] Yes, because all it took was one phone call to have someone give you money.

Leaving the Streets

The narratives of young adults and adolescents consistently demonstrate that life on the street is not often pleasant. The poverty, violence and nature of the relationships endured by those who are sexually exploited create a situation that most would wish to escape. McIntyre noted that almost all of the fifty sex workers that she interviewed had a plan to exit. These plans were "a mechanism to erase the pain and frustration associated with sex work.... Although this appears as a contradiction on the surface, it is an important feature in allowing a sex worker to continue this work, knowing that it is not permanent" (1999: 171). Despite having a plan, though, most of McIntyre's respondents did not leave permanently, either as adolescents or adults. This is consistent with other researchers who have reported that exiting from the street is difficult.

About two-thirds of the women whom we interviewed had left the streets, with two women still prostituting occasionally. The Aboriginal participants were significantly more likely to be still working (thirteen of seventeen) than those of Caucasian origin.

As adolescents, almost all the women had attempted to leave prostitution at least once. Most of the attempts to exit occurred after a significant or traumatic event. Several women attempted to leave after they became pregnant; others quit after a bad date or after they were arrested.

> After [being beaten by a john], we didn't want to take any chances, because I have a kid and the thought of losing your kid, going out one night and not coming back and your kid's wondering, "Where's mommy?"

> I don't work no more because I have my son and you never know if you are going to end up in jail or get a bad date and end up in the hospital.

> I never want to be in that little jail cell. I never want to be handcuffed again; it was a very intimidating process for me. But that lock up experience was what did it for me. I was sort of scared straight.

Others wished to prevent child protection services from apprehending their children or they realized that their lifestyle was detrimental to their children's welfare. For several, becoming pregnant, either as teens or as adults, became their *raison d'être* for leaving. As noted by one mother, "I just finally woke up. I have three kids, pregnant with him [pointing to infant], and it was just the same shit every friggin day—go to work, come home. And it really looked like it was compromising my parenting skills."

Although almost all attempted to exit, the majority returned to working, primarily for financial reasons. Some admitted returning to prostitution because they needed money for their drug addiction. Despite good intentions it was often difficult to maintain their resolve to exit permanently. As one women related:

> Getting pregnant fixed me. I knew I had to change. It helped me grow up a lot. That's not to say I didn't [go back] once he turned about six months old. I had been completely sober, radically against drugs and alcohol. I swore when I got pregnant that there was no way I was going to give my kid a hard life. I was going to take care of him. I was so powerless once I started drinking, doing drugs and sleeping with all these guys again.

Numerous women returned because of what they termed their addiction to the money and to the street: This seemed a more feasible alternative than working at a low paying job where they would have to wait to get their pay cheque. One woman commented that, "I wanted to leave, but the money was there. I hated to leave because I was used to having so much money in the day." Another stated, "That's easy money. If I went out there right now I'd be guaranteed in half an hour to have fifty bucks in my pocket."

The term "easy money" is a debatable one, especially in light of the extent of violence and the common wish to exit. Almost half of the women noted that prostitution is a means of survival and that they need the money. This was a major factor in their staying involved: to buy groceries, feed and clothe their children and pay the rent. One woman commented, "I don't think people see why we go out on the street. A lot of time we have no other way of getting money. It's degrading, but I would rather make sure that my daughter has food than worry about myself." Another reflected, "If I didn't make any money I had nowhere to sleep. I had to blow the hotel owner just to have a bed." A third noted, "I had to go back to the stroll to pay rent."

A relatively small number of women made no attempt to leave prostitution. They described several barriers that prevented them from even considering leaving. Interestingly, several saw it as part of their identity (as discussed in Chapter Two)—that was simply who they were. One woman noted, "I started when I was so young, it's just been part of my life. It's not out of the ordinary." Another commented, "Prostitution is an addiction all in itself. I can't explain it. I mean there's just the excitement of being down there. That was my life; that was my family." A third woman reflected that, "It's hard to get out. When I walk down the street guys still try to pick me up. I try and avoid it and deny I did it. But deep down I still have my guilty feeling of working the streets."

Only eight of the thirty women who have now exited left for good when they were adolescents. Of these, several mentioned that formal programs assisted them to leave. At age seventeen, one young woman received support from a specialized service for adolescents exploited through prostitution and then went to a substance rehabilitation centre, "I thought I'll do this rehab thing, go there and when I get out, I'll make my decisions then. I'll have a clear head. And when I got out, I just didn't want it anymore." Since leaving is a complex process, many factors influence whether the decision to leave will be permanent. This woman also noted that her boyfriend supported her leaving.

As adolescents, two young women spent time in jail and were connected to supportive services during or afterwards. One of these commented, "The [police] arrested me, I got a criminal record. I have to wait until I'm twenty-three to get a pardon. That did it for me!" She also received assistance from a street outreach agency that helped her get out of jail.

Another woman described hitting rock bottom before she left as a teen. She and a girlfriend had been arrested and put in jail for two weeks. "Things just started to make sense. I started thinking there has got to be more to life than this. People around me were dying." She mentioned how important it was that her mother remained supportive, "I think she really helped me get off the street because she stopped trying to control me. She always told me that she loved me, that she would be there for me when I'm ready ... just re-affirming that I'd have her there when I was ready."

Other women who left while under age eighteen also mentioned personal reasons (the involvement of family or promising a boyfriend to stop) as helping them to successfully exit. "It just lasted a few weeks. My mom found out and she came and got me." The difficulty and the complexity of leaving, especially when still an adolescent, is perhaps best exemplified by the following quote:

> Every agency in the city had given up on me. That was a big pointer [to], "I might want to get my shit together." Every agency in the city was saying, "I'm sorry; we can't deal with you anymore. We've tried and tried and tried. Sorry, we've heard this too many times." I've told them too many times that, "Oh, I want to get off." And gone back.

Concluding Thoughts

The women's stories are graphic portrayals of their lives and struggles. The narratives reveal complex and difficult lives characterized by poverty, violence, control by others and a failure of society's traditional institutions to assist children. As young teens, few had supportive families and all were vulnerable as a result of either having run away from institutions or dysfunctional families or of living in disadvantaged surroundings (see also Biehal and Wade 1999).

The fact that, on first becoming sexually exploited through prostitution, Aboriginal girls were more likely to be living at home and Caucasian girls more likely to have run away from their families or child welfare placement has not been previously highlighted. Both groups of children experienced poverty that became a factor in their entry into prostitution. As the Royal Commission on Aboriginal Peoples in 1996 noted that: "It has been estimated that 50 percent of Aboriginal children, whether living on or off reserve, are living in poverty" (RCAP 1996: 169). Similarly, while it is not clear why the majority of the women we interviewed who were still involved in prostitution were Aboriginal, poverty is a likely factor.

Most of the women with whom we spoke were primarily prostituting on the streets. Both the Aboriginal and Caucasian women repeatedly commented about returning to, or staying in, prostitution for money for survival—being able to pay the rent or buy groceries—echoing their initial reasons for becoming involved. As adolescents, they often had little choice in this, although several noted that, as adults, they moved into more mainstream agencies such as escort services or massage parlours, in which hiring underage adolescents is illegal. Acknowledging and addressing the disproportionate poverty of Aboriginal Canadians through policy changes and an influx of financial support could thus have as one of its benefits the prevention of sexual exploitation of girls and young women who prostitute themselves as a means to meet their basic needs.

Prevention strategies may be different for Aboriginal as compared to Caucasian girls. A community approach, involving elders and local women and men who have experienced the perils of the streets, may be well-suited for Aboriginal populations. In the case of both Caucasian and Aboriginal young women, targeting those taken into care by the child welfare system or those at risk of such care would be a better approach than universal school programs.

While most of the women were involved with pimps at some point, sometimes through coercion, sometimes by choice, many did not have a pimp for long periods, maintaining independent control of their activities. Some were trafficked across the country by pimps, although other women travelled by choice. The narrow line between intimate partners or boyfriends and pimps, as has been documented previously (Dalla 2002), was also apparent. Many had partners who would send them out on the streets, yet the women did not necessarily perceive them as pimps.

The use of substances by those sexually exploited by prostitution has been well-documented. Here, as elsewhere, it is a frequently cited reason for needing money that can lead to the initial entry, although the larger context of their lives and the need to survive on the streets were also central. Once on the streets, a number of the women ultimately used significantly addictive drugs such as crack cocaine and heroin, a serious factor in preventing their exit (see also Young et al. 2000). Although many entered prostitution to finance drug use, the increasing severity of their substance abuse is likely caused by the distress associated with their involvement in prostitution.

The women's narratives with respect to their histories of child sexual abuse, involvement with child welfare agencies and the mechanics of entry including "survival sex" and poverty are similar to those documented elsewhere (Estes 2001; Kingsley and Mark 2000; McIntyre

1999; Tyler, Hoyt, Whitbeck and Cauce 2001). Their stories highlight the difficulty of leaving, especially once one is entrenched in substance abuse and has developed a support network of others also involved in prostitution. Even having a number of children taken into care or having supportive family or partners did not prevent some women from remaining on or returning to the streets (see also Dalla 2001).

We still know little about what services could assist adolescents wishing to leave (Arnold et al. 2000; Cauce et al. 1998). Given the extent to which the women spoke of both wishing to leave as teens and their lack of success (see also McIntyre 1999; Unger et al. 1998), the need for effective and appropriate services to assist young street-involved women is clear, and is the focus of Chapter Six in this book.

Chapter Two

"The People We Think We Are"
The Social Identities of Girls Involved in Prostitution

Pamela Downe with "Ashley-Mika"

Introduction

When I first met "Ashley-Mika"[1] in 1998, she had just turned sixteen, though at the time she told me (and I believed her) that she was almost nineteen. She later explained that she thought an adult would never take her seriously if she revealed her younger age. Having heard of my research with sexually exploited youth in Central America, Ashley-Mika had come to my university office to seek my help because she and several of her friends wanted to do something (although they were not yet sure what) to help inform other young street-involved women and men about the hardships that often accompany an involvement in prostitution. Ashley-Mika knows these hardships well; since she was twelve years old, she has been exploited through prostitution. Three years after her initial involvement—which began when she ran away from an abusive home and met an even more abusive pimp—she felt the need to speak out about her experiences, but because of her ongoing exploitation, she wanted to choose her venues carefully. She temporarily participated in efforts to develop a PEERS (Prostitute Empowerment and Education Resource Services) centre in Saskatoon, but she became frustrated by, in her words, "the identity politics" that she believed were thwarting this initiative. "The escort girls[2] want it one way, the Indians want it another, us Metis want it another, and the White girls [want] ... to run the show," she explained. "Like, we all have our ideas based, you know, on what we've gone through and, like, the people we think we are." This last phrase caught my attention: "the people we think we are." For young women like Ashley-Mika, what informs such thinking?

The purpose of this chapter is to present an overview of how the women participating in this study spoke about themselves, their public and private identities, as well as the world around them, in light of their involvement in systems of prostitution.[3] This inquiry is not only critical to our understanding of the effects of children's sexual exploitation, but it is also highly relevant to any examination of policies and programming concerning prostitution and exploited youth. Many researchers and activists have argued that young women who are sexually exploited through prostitution tend to have a "poorly experienced and underdeveloped sense of personal power ... a deep feeling of being inconsequential to anyone or anything" (McMullen 1987: 39). As such, they turn to street communities, drugs, pimps and dealers to develop personal identities and an enduring sense of place and belonging. While many service providers with whom we spoke admirably and impressively described the need for non-judgmental care and programs that "accept the girls for who they are," we should first know how these young women's identities are constructed and who they know themselves to be. Operating on preconceived ideas of who sexually exploited youth are can be detrimental to the overall success of even the best designed programs or policies. In this chapter, I outline some of the major influences that inform how the forty-seven women interviewed constructed self-identities while involved in prostitution. The implications of this analysis, however, extend beyond the specificities of this project in that they reflect broader social influences of racism, sexism, class- and age-based hierarchies that surely affect the identity formation of most—if not all—youth in Canada.

Self identities function in very fundamental and intimate ways—both socially and individually—to inform our actions and our thoughts, and they therefore must be taken into consideration when assessing the extent and significance of sexual exploitation. Psychologists have long argued that childhood is a pivotal time for the development of identity, and it is clear from our research that there are numerous influencing factors that shape how exploited youth see themselves and how they situate themselves in the world around them. These influencing factors include (1) how the exploited youth relate to prostitution (that is, what the word "prostitution" means to them and how they embody various identities that link or separate them from prostitution); (2) a presiding fear; (3) drug use and addiction; (4) social networks; (5) age, gender and cultural heritage; and (6) motherhood. Identities cannot be easily reduced to single influences (such as relationships with parents, instances of abuse or peer groups); rather, self-identities are crafted from a complex mixing of these various influences that shape who we are and who we hope to be.

What Does the Word "Prostitution" Mean to You?
"Nothing, Because You Are Nothing"

The majority of the women interviewed clearly defined prostitution as something unique—always different and usually deviant—that set them apart from other children and youth of similar age. At the same time and somewhat contradictorily, prostitution was also seen as simply an everyday and routine way of relating to the world. As one young woman said,

> I've been doing it so long now, for me it's long 'cause you know I started when I was so young, it's just been, just a part of my life sort of thing. It's not even something that's out of the ordinary.

Sociologically, then, prostitution was seen as being both a marker of difference and an unremarkable and routine experience for those involved in it.

When asked what the word "prostitution" means, the women offered a variety of answers ranging from simple explanations of "sex for money" to more complicated and reflective accounts of street cultures, social networks and sexual encounters. These answers were elaborated further throughout the interviews, and a series of characteristic but contrasting pictures were revealed. Perhaps the most apparent contrast was between images of degradation and images of glamour. One young woman, for example, reduced herself to nothing through her affiliation with prostitution when she explained that "[prostitution] means nothing, because you are nothing." Echoing that deprecatory tone, another woman explained that her involvement in prostitution was the lowest point in her life. Her child had been taken from her and she explained:

> I lost it. I mean, I didn't have anything to feel guilty about anymore, you know. I didn't have anybody to come home to…. So, for months I degraded myself in every and any way possible. I set about underpricing myself and … I hit bottom.

Statements such as these can be contrasted with the romanticized pictures of "glitz, glamour and easy money" that were painted by other women who recounted their street involvement. Referring to her second venture into prostitution, one young woman recalled the following,

> At that point in time, it was the glitter and glamour of prostitution. All the girls in the $600 boots, and you know, all the fur coats and blah, blah, blah…. I can make fifty bucks pan-handling in one night or I can make 600 bucks on the street, you know.

Another woman agreed, saying, "I thought, 'money, cool! I want to be like that.' You know, I saw these girls wearing fur coats and I thought they were cool."

These images of degradation and decadent glamour are critically important to how young women exploited through prostitution see themselves and how they present themselves to others because such images create two contrasting points with which the young women we interviewed identify. Seeing themselves as either degraded or glamorous—or, as I discuss momentarily, a combination of both—has great influence on issues of self-esteem and receptivity to available voluntary and mandated programs. However, the contrast between these images was not always clear-cut. One woman began by explaining that being a prostitute was actually something she *wanted* to be because she initially held a quite positive view of commercialized sex:

> When I started fixing drugs it was, like, "I want to work the streets. I want to be a prostitute. I want to make money for this." And I knew I could do it because I was so dissociated from my body.... My body was just a tool and having sex with people was not anything I even batted an eye at.

As she continued her story, though, it was clear that the glamorous image and allure of prostitution became increasingly tarnished as she encountered more negative experiences. After two particularly violent episodes with clients, she re-assessed her opinion:

> I thought, like, this is a really crappy way to live my life. I'm not having a good time here. So those two incidents started me thinking that maybe this isn't as glamorous and as wonderful as I originally thought it would be.... [But] prostitution is addictive and ... it took me a long time to get it out of my head that [I] could go back and work the street.

Eventually, her initial abilities to dissociate psychologically from what was happening to her body failed her and she ultimately identified herself in a very negative and lasting way with prostitution:

> Without a career, without that stability of a solid education and career, I'm nothing but some ... whore with no place to live. To this day, I still see myself in those roles quite often [and I] have trouble overcoming that.

There are many interesting facets to this woman's story, including the implicit contrast between prostitution as a source of production (primarily financial production) and prostitution as a site of loss. Several of the women interviewed, as noted above, were quick to equate prostitution with money, and they clearly saw selling sex as a source of relative wealth, as an activity that ultimately gives more than it takes. For these women, prostitution provided money for subsistence and drugs, but it also gave them something more. Prostitution was sometimes seen—usually only fleetingly, though—as a source of otherwise unavailable opportunities, such as travel and pride:

> When I was about sixteen to eighteen, that's when it was, like, I was a ho'. There is no ifs, ands, or buts about it, no denying it to anyone. I was proud of the fact I was a prostitute. You know, umm, I went to Montreal for six months, I'd come back. I went to Vancouver for a couple of weeks, I came back. I went to Calgary for a little bit and I came back. I went to Edmonton then I came back.

In addition to money and occasional travel, street involvement also provided a sense of belonging and an accepting social environment that the women participating in this research had rarely experienced elsewhere. Sexual exploitation through prostitution was a small price to pay in exchange for that sense of community and the cultural currency that led them to feel as though they belonged somewhere. Kingsley and Mark (2000: 33) argue that it is in the last stage of involvement in prostitution where association is virtually exclusively with others in the sex trade and where those identifying as "prostitutes" find themselves accepted. The end result for those involved is a feeling of belonging and community that fills the emotional gaps often created in a childhood marked by abuse and abandonment, and that also makes it difficult to exit:

> There's that sense of addiction to the streets, [it] is also addiction to other people on the streets because of the fact that they know who you are. You don't have to hide you're a prostitute. If I went and saw any of my old friends, there was always, "Oh well, you know, what are you doing now?" Well, you'd lie, you know. And it's hard to live off lies because you get caught in lies and when you're on the streets, you don't need to lie. There's no reason for it … you're accepted.

Such feelings and experiences of belonging and acceptance have been shown, time and time again, to be critically influential in the psychological and social development of children and youth (e.g., Downe 1998; Veale, Taylor and Linehan 2000). It is from a sense of belonging that a sense of personal identity emerges, often so strongly that youth have a difficult time seeing themselves or experiencing the world around them in other ways. The following interview excerpt illustrates this well. This young woman had a long history of involvement in prostitution and she saw her involvement as part and parcel of the broader street culture to which she belonged. When she was repeatedly confronted and antagonized by school mates for wearing conflicting gang colours, thereby making her place in the school-related social networks unclear, she was confused, ultimately arguing that her allegiance was to the street and to being a "street kid":

> The other girls at school would say "I'm hearing that you're down with [name]." "Oh well, I'm hearing you're down with both [name] and [name] but you can't be down with both." And it's like, "who the hell are you hearing your information from, girl?" I like, God, I hang around (the street) for Christ sake. I'm a street kid.… There's your answer, I'm a street kid. There.

From very specific references to being a prostitute on the street to more ambiguous references to street culture and being a "street kid," there are many examples of how street cultures create contexts for young women to gain a sense of belonging at the same time as they construct a sense of self and identity. Getting out of prostitution, taking steps to end the ongoing sexual exploitation and asking for assistance, then, can seem insurmountable and even unimaginable for these vulnerable youth whose very sense of belonging is so rooted in street cultures and systems of prostitution. However, set against such strong recollections of community, are equally strong stories of loss, embarrassment and abuse. Our research also shows that as powerful a pull as the money and sense of belonging may be, an ongoing sense of loss often counters it. In prostitution, loss takes many forms. For the women participating in this study, embarrassment, the loss of pride, the removal of children from their care, a persistent lack of safety and the death of friends or family are the most common types. Many of these losses will be discussed in later sections of this chapter as well as elsewhere in this volume. When taken together, however, these losses create "a cycle just like an abusive relationship. It keeps going and going. It's a cycle of being afraid," as one woman explained. Her reference to fear is apt, for it figures very prominently in the women's recollections of their involvement in prostitution, and fear has had a lasting effect on many of them.

Fear: "I Was Sort of Scared Straight"

Patricia Marquez (1999) notes that fear permeates the prevailing atmosphere of the streets as well as many treatment facilities. Our interviews with both service providers and the youth support this observation. The women with whom we spoke were strongly affected by the presiding fear of loss, abuse, disease and even death that characterizes this kind of sexual exploitation. For them, fear was something that they not only dealt with on a daily basis, but it came to define their moods, dictate their movements and influence how they related to others. Fear, then, had a great impact on how the women saw (and in some cases continue to see) themselves and their place in the world. The importance of fear as an influencing factor in the young women's lives was also recognized by the service providers who spoke repeatedly about the need to create and offer *safe* places for sexually exploited youth. The service providers argued that these places should offer not only respite from specific sources of fear (such as police harassment, arrest or abusive pimps and clients) but also relief from the general and often unspecified trepidation that characterizes street communities.

Although individual sources of fear could be itemized, general references to an overall context of trepidation were more likely to spontaneously emerge in our discussions. As one young woman re-marked,

> The whole scenario ... was very scary, not knowing anything about what could or should happen.... So one night turned into two nights, and two nights turned into a week, and a few months later, he [her pimp] became violent toward me and I pressed charges.... It was very scary....The cops were very pushy and stuff.

In fact, references to fearfulness were all-encompassing:

> I knew I would end up on the street. As soon as that night when I was there and was drugged up, the next night, I was on the street. I knew there was no turning back, I knew I would be out there.... I was scared. I was fourteen years old. You're not going to say no to some guy who is twice your age.

For many of the women, the fear they felt while working on the streets was a continuation, albeit in a different form, of the fear they experienced in their own homes. One young woman contrasted the insecurity and uncertainty that she felt in her own home while her alcoholic stepfather sexually abused her with what her mother must have felt at the same time, "[Mother] doesn't know half of the stuff because she was always at work.... Living with an alcoholic as an adult is less fearful because you always feel you have a choice." She implies here that the lack of choice that emerged from this abusive situation led to feelings of fear. A similar lack of choice characterized her involvement in prostitution and garnered a similar but intensified kind of fear. Another woman who also faced ongoing sexual abuse in her home as a child made a similar comment, "[Prostituting] myself was easy and scary to do.... It was happening at home anyways. What was the difference?" A continuum between a home- and street-based fear and abuse is therefore established and clearly illustrates how this emotion was (and for others still is) a routine fixture in the lives of these young women. Fear indelibly marked the identities of many of the women, creating a lack of trust and a sense of insecurity. As one young woman said, "I'm not a bad person. I'm who I am now because of what I was before, [but] ... it's made me a very untrusting person, unfortunately."

Although fear is so commonplace for sexually exploited youth, it was recognized by most of the women we interviewed as being a powerful motivator for change. In fact, most of the women repeatedly claimed that moments of intense fearfulness were turning points for them, and many made decisions to change the extent or nature of their involvement in prostitution as a result. One young woman was so familiar with the power of fear to alter one's course in prostitution that she and her friends would use it to deter other young women on the streets:

> If we were working and we see somebody under eighteen, we wouldn't beat them up, we would go up to them and scare them and say, get out of here before we do something to you. That's the only way that they will get off. They get scared. Trust me, when I was fourteen, I got scared a few times.

While women made comments such as this about the way fear on the streets can be used as a deterrent for other girls, most of the reported moments of intense fear had something to do with the legal system:

> ... this is probably the most intimidating experience of my life was being in the cells in the court house. They're very small and there's writing on the walls.... And reading all that writing on the walls and thinking about the people that had been in this room before me, and I was so scared. And I wanted to be out so badly.

Obviously, this woman's awareness that she was part of a larger but anonymous group of people who had passed through the courthouse cells was a turning point. It is as if the street communities on which she relied lost their aura of trustworthiness as she thought about the large numbers of people involved with the judicial system. Street communities along with the drug networks and systems of prostitution became risk factors and liabilities, not a collective source of acceptance. She continued to explain,

> That lock up experience was what did it for me. I was sort of scared straight.... It made a transformation in that, OK, I'm going to get out of hooking and, umm, quit drugs.... I knew there that I'm really failing in life here.

Fear, therefore, was not only a negative influence on the women while they were involved in prostitution, it was also what motivated them to leave, to change their life decisions. When asked for ideas about how girls can be dissuaded from continuing their involvement in prostitution, one woman offered the following advice:

> I would say scare them. Scare them into seeing that you go out and deal with stinky old men and people who are really sick. The diseases, the problems ... you could lose your family that way. People don't look at it like a problem, but it is a problem.

We heard many similar suggestions. To redress this problem, a problem that too often persists with indemnity, many of the women with whom we spoke suggested that girls involved in prostitution need to be "scared straight." The phrasing here is telling. It refers both to the ever-present fear that characterizes street life and to the need to "straighten" what is askew, namely ongoing sexual abuse and drug use. But "straightening out" was more difficult than many of the participants in this study thought it would be; for others, it remains a difficult and yet unachieved task. This is largely because of the effects of ongoing and recurrent drug use and addictions.

Drug Use: "Being High Means Up Tall, Not Whore and Small"

For most of the women, prostitution and drug use were intimately connected. Indeed, this connection figured centrally in the vast majority of interviews and it became clear that to examine how prostitution informs the social identities of the women and girls involved in it requires that we examine the same for drug use. Perhaps the best way to understand these influences is to explore how involvement in prostitution is equated with drug use. One young woman explained:

> If I quit drugs, I quit ho'-ing.... And if I go out to work, I've actually tried this, going out [because] I need $40 worth of groceries ... [and] I'm going to go out and make a quick twenty bucks so I can buy groceries. And once I have that $20, which is never ... because I don't want to sell myself for twenty bucks, then I've got enough for rock. And I'm going to get that rock thinking "well, I

can just [make] the money back again, and I'm up for eight days chasing it. And if I have money, and I smoke cocaine … then when the cocaine is gone [and] I have no more money left I'm going to go out and ho'…. They're connected for me.

Yet another woman described the connection between an involvement in prostitution and drug use as cyclical:

Like, the only times I really, like, seriously worked the streets, was like when I was using needle drugs. And then, you know, I wanted it all the time, so I'd be, you know, going out, grabbing,[4] coming home, getting high, going out, grabbing, coming home, getting high, twenty-four/seven kind of thing.

In these characteristic explanations of prostitution and drug use, the lines between the two activities become blurred. Drug use and selling sex are intertwined, two sides of the same coin. Indisputably, these combined activities, and all the abuses that accompany them, contributed to how the women saw themselves and presented themselves to the world. Often, they identified as an "addict," an identity that they saw as primarily biological and engulfing. One woman, for example, explained that the difficulties she had in fitting into her adoptive family were a direct result of being "born" an addict: "I was just addicted, born addicted or whatever." Another made a similar comment when she eschewed explanations that her drug use was a coping strategy and instead offered a description of herself as a natural addict, saying "I had an abortion and that led to more drugs because I didn't know how to cope with it. That's what they tell me anyways. But I think I'm just an addict, born an addict." Drugs, like being sexually exploited for money, are not only activities that are performed, they are activities that define who the women were and, in some cases, are. The women who described themselves as addicts were most likely to describe frustration over the inescapability of the cycles of drug- and sexual-abuse. For example, when asked if her children know that she does drugs or is involved in prostitution, one young woman ultimately described herself as being "stuck" in a cycle that is directly the result of who she is and what she does:

[My kids] are too young to know nothing. I love them. But, you know, this is what I do. It's who I am. I can't get off the drugs. I don't want to get off the drugs and, like, I mean I can't give the kids away, eh. I can't get away from the whole [prostitution and drug] thing so, like, I'm totally stuck.

Other women were less likely to see their drug use as contributing to their vulnerability but instead used drugs as a way to cope with that vulnerability. Rather than referring to themselves as "addicts" and recounting the perceived inescapability of their situation, these women were more likely to see themselves as drug users. For them, drug use was recreational, and, in the context of their involvement in prostitution, therapeutic in that it helped numb them to the exploitation, violence and resulting degradation that they often experienced. One woman put it very well when she said, "It sounds bad, or whatever, but ... I forget all the ho' shit when I'm high. Being high means up tall, not whore and small." Drug use, then was a way for this young woman to feel better about herself, to situate herself in contrast to the degrading image of "whore." Another woman agreed, arguing that it is virtually impossible for her to face the exploitation she is exposed to without anaesthetizing herself with drugs and alcohol:

> Sometimes you have to be stoned drunk to do it.... I was on alcohol and on coke last year. I spent maybe three weeks on it at a different time.... It's just that you can't face [the] reality of doing it when you're straight. You have to be stoned out of your tree. I find that I have to be spooked right out of my tree to be doing this.

Still another woman found the sexual abuse and exploitation of prostitution so unnerving that she drank and took prescription pills every day, "so I wouldn't feel nothing. It was awful. Like, I needed something."

For some women, the drugs that they used as a coping mechanism became a source of support and pride. One participant, who survived an abusive home and several violent johns, even referred to her drug use as a "badge of honour":

> The drugs made me happy.... Drugs was my new mission statement. But, like, alcohol doesn't work for me, and I'm just going to obliviate myself. I'm going to do drugs as much as I can. And it was like a badge of honour that I wore. I'm going to be the biggest stonehead I can. And, umm, I had some fun. I went on a lot of trips.

Drugs, then, provided a source of pride for this woman who went on to say that her ability to be a prolific and efficient drug user set her apart from the others—the "junkies"—with whom she associated. Like the woman who said being high meant being "tall, not whore and small," this young woman similarly used her drug use to create a more positive self identity, one that allowed her to reject the label "junkie" and position herself "above" others around her:

> I felt that, you know, I was hanging around with people that were less than me. I felt better than these people, and I felt better than all the tricks, and I felt better than the people I was living with that were fixing me up because they were junkies and I wasn't a junkie. So I was better than them. They adored me, and ... the tricks I had sex with, they adored me. Some of them came back specifically to look for me.

The effectiveness of drugs as either an informal anesthetic to the exploitation of prostitution or a "badge of honour," however, was very often fleeting, as an equal number of women recalled the vulnerability that resulted from ongoing drug use. Persistent drug use was often the reason that the women lost custody of their children. Drug use was blamed for the loss of friendships, family support and employment. And drug use was often described as underlying the abusive relationships with boyfriends and pimps. One woman, who moved to northern Manitoba to get away from an abusive relationship, described this vulnerability well, saying,

> It was fear, what made me get off drugs. It wasn't that I wanted to be off them. Really. 'Cause I still wanted to use. I still had tremendous cravings for them and I tried to access it in [the northern city] but I couldn't get it. But yeah, the fear of coming back to [an abusive ex-boyfriend]. The only reason I'm back now is I know him and another guy are gone.

This narrative reveals an interesting and significant shift from a very clear discussion of drugs and drug use to an equally clear description of her ex-boyfriend and the fear that resulted from ongoing abuse. A similar kind of shift from references to violence and drugs to people occurred when one woman referred to her abusive pimp as being the same as the drug to which she was addicted:

> When we fight back, it just makes it worse. There's not no place we can go to get nobody to do shit about it. [I've been with him] about two years. Yeah, two years, I guess. I mean, I suppose I could, like, leave but he's my hookup. He's how I get the crack, eh. And he's always got some. He's, like, never without it. He's, like, the same as the drug, you know.

In this case, the man became equated with the drug. Another woman conversely personified her drug as a pimp, saying, "My drug is my pimp.... I work for it, I can't live without it. My drug is my pimp, yeah."

The results of our interviews therefore clearly suggest that the drugs, people and places associated with systems of prostitution are equated with each other. Addiction, therefore, refers to pathological drug dependence but it also refers to the entire community context that informs how these women see themselves and others.

Social Network: Pimps, Partners, Pals and Parents

Social identities are not created in individual vacuums but through interactions with others. Family members, boyfriends, pimps and friends were the primary groups with or against which the women affiliated themselves as they crafted social identities as prostituted youth. Sometimes the references to this prevailing social network were very direct and down-to-earth. They were neither dramatic nor startling and they demonstrated how truly routine and taken-for-granted these social networks were. One woman, for example, simply described street life by describing her friends:

> I was friends with all the girls. The one girl I was telling you about ... she is one of my best friends. We were working and we were also having fun together at the same time. And we had a friendship. If we got bored, we would walk to the park and we would go to the bar and have lunch.

Another woman made similarly insightful but not necessarily astonishing comments about her extended street network, saying, "It's true, because you have everybody down there.... They help each other out. I'll be honest, I feel safer down there than by my place, just because I know everybody." This place where "everybody knows your name," to borrow the cliché reference to the television *Cheers* bar, which Ashley-Mika often used, became akin to family, and the women relied on it as such.

Although it was not common, street families and families of origin occasionally overlapped and together constituted a fairly extensive social network. When asked what she would do if she were ever in trouble, one woman said,

> I would mostly have to call on street people, like if I had a bad date or something. Then I'd go get like a bro' or something and go get him to, ah, you know finish it off or whatever. Or if I, if something happened, like between me and another street person, or other street people, then, you know, [I] would have to get some of my relatives involved. 'Cause, you know, if you get in trouble like that it's usually, it would have to be something big.

For this woman, there were distinctions between family members and street friends, but these distinctions were not barriers. This confidence in family and the integration of family members into street communities, however, are actually quite unusual. While there were exceptions, the vast majority of the women had very little to do with their families of origin.

Families of origin were often invoked in the interviews as explanations for why the women became involved in drug use and prostitution in the first place. Speaking broadly, one woman believes that, when families do not provide adequate support or nurturing, a sense of vulnerability and lack of self confidence results:

> A lot of street kids grow up with no parents really.... Being a child and then growing up knowing that you're somebody but not really learning that.... You need [to know] you're, like, really a somebody.

Others spoke more directly and personally about the abuse that led them to the street and that precluded any further contact with family members:

> [My stepfather] didn't mean to be mean. He was drunk and he was bitter and he needed to have power over somebody. He dominated over me and my brothers.... He was never physically or sexually abusive towards me, but the emotional abuse was extreme.

What is interesting is that same sense of neglect and abuse that characterized the women's experiences in their families, also tends to characterize their relationships with their pimps. Yet pimps often remain central to the street communities and social networks while family members are, for the most part, estranged.

While many women reported working without pimps, most had at one time or another been associated with one. Similarly, while there is no consistency in the influence that the women acknowledge the pimps to have on their lives, there is no doubt that the women's encounters with these mostly male managers have a discernible effect on the crafting of social identities. As illustrated by the following interview excerpt, pimps are often the central figures in facilitating the young women's activities in prostitution:

> I could not tell you why but one night I decided I wanted to go back to work. I went out and I knew this one pimp ... because my friend was working for him and so I knew him already. I literally walked up to him and said, "I want to start working again."

Not only was her involvement in prostitution facilitated by this pimp, but it was clear that he, like other pimps, held a central place in determining who worked the streets and under what conditions. Even women who reported having peripheral or no relationship with the pimps were ultimately affected by them and the position they held in the street culture. One woman explained that even though she did not admittedly work explicitly for the pimps (one of whom was a woman) with whom she was living, she still needed to use their names to gain respect:

> The three of us were living off my earnings. And that was OK with me because they gave me a place to live and they loved me and adored me....He wasn't really my pimp, and she wasn't really my pimp, and I didn't really have a pimp, but I used their name because you needed, I was told I needed to have the name to work this corner.... They told me that I needed to work this corner.

Despite her claims of autonomy, her roommates had noticeable control over her movement, money and perhaps even her mind-set at the time. This kind of coercion and exploitation kept her well within a circum-scribed role, one which she found satisfying at the time, but one that also reflected the hierarchies that inform how the women can and cannot position and represent themselves in prevailing street cultures.

Just as enticing images of prostitution generally were offset by more devastating experiences of loss, positive images of a supportive social network were also countered with stories of betrayal, fear of abuse and recognized exploitation. This is particularly true in discussions of pimps. When asked about the Alberta-based Protection of Children Involved in Prostitution legislation, one woman replied,

> If an under aged girl is working for a pimp and you yank her off the street for seventy-two hours and then you let her go and of course she's going to go back to her pimp. Hello? Right, she's going to get the beating of her life, you know. And I know enough girls who have gone back to their pimp and got the shit kicked out of them for being gone two hours, never mind three days.

Evidently, pimps and occasionally drug dealers became embodiments of abuse. Social street networks, therefore, were not consistently support-ive or accepting; they were just as likely to be devastating and threaten-ing in ways that had a lasting impact.

The positive relationships that were and are forged through systems of prostitution tend to be with other experiential youth, and occasionally with dedicated counsellors and outreach workers. As discussed in Chapter Six, these relationships were pivotal for those women who decided to exit prostitution and to tackle addiction problems. One young woman echoed the sentiments of many when she explained, "I believe if you're going to, you know, get off the road, if you have friends you'll get off through talking with other people, other friends." Indeed, in recounting the successful efforts to quit drugs and to extricate themselves from an engulfing street culture most women claimed that their success was attributable to having friends to support them like they did while working the streets. At the same time, the lure of the streets is always there to be resisted. Given that the extended social network provides an environment that informs each woman's sense of self and social place, resistance can be difficult. As one woman said,

> I have become friends with a lot of people down there. I'm pretty well-known down there now. That's why I want to stay away from there. I have quit and gone back, quite a few times, actually. What drives me back is being around there. I used to choose to live around there, around that area that's [got] good access to … the street. But it's not a good idea for me at all, that's why I'm choosing to move away from that whole area.… I'm very vulnerable to it, not the drinking. It's not so much the drinking, it's that I want to be around those people because sometimes I feel lonely … and sometimes it's just to fit in.

Programs designed to assist youth in getting off the streets and making a new start need to provide opportunities where supportive and complex relationships akin to street relationships can be cultivated, but in contexts that promote self-confidence rather than exploitation. It is clear that many service providers are well aware of this but they often argue that is the hardest part. We are, after all, trying to replace years of social networks that not only functioned as a background to these young women's activities but informed how these women situated themselves in the world.

Age, Gender and Cultural Heritage: "I Was Blond. I Was White. I Was Sixteen. I Was … Prime"

As in identity construction generally, age, gender and cultural heritage play an important role in identity construction of street youth. In prevailing social theories of identity, these factors are perhaps among the most frequently discussed (e.g., James and Shadd 2001). Although the women participating in this study rarely made explicit references to how their cultural heritage or gender affected their involvement in prostitution, our research suggests that the Aboriginal women were more likely to set themselves apart from the non-Aboriginal women. In very significant ways, Aboriginal women stressed the difficulty they had in finding a place in a dominant and decidedly racist society. For example, when one young Aboriginal woman finally met her birth mother, after having had a hard time fitting into her adoptive family, she said,

> It helped with identity a lot. Because ... that really bothered me.... Like, I look White but I knew I was Indian. And I didn't fit with the White people, [but I] didn't fit with the Indians either. But now I know who I am.

Referring, then, to a very essentialist understanding of Aboriginality, this woman described quite clearly what some of the other Aboriginal women only suggested: "fitting in" is more difficult and ultimately more deleterious to one's sense of self when there is such ambiguity and ambivalence about where you belong. While such sentiments are often expressed by people of Aboriginal heritage, we must consider such comments seriously because the women clearly linked these culturally and family-based identity issues with their exploitation through prostitution as well as with programs that are designed to assist them. Another young woman, for example, was adamant that a newly formed support group for Metis women involved in prostitution would be more successful than past efforts because it was designed specifically for those of Metis heritage:

> It's not, like, it's not, you know, so much of the programs as it is being with other people who you can talk to and, you know, not be so ashamed or whatever. It's like having people like me there, you know.... [It] gives me somewheres to go. It's for us Metis women.

Very few of the non-Aboriginal women whom we interviewed made explicit reference to their cultural heritage, although references to religion did occasionally arise throughout the course of our discussions. One woman, for instance, described the difficulties she had accepting her parents' staunch Christianity, saying,

> [My relationship with my parents] was pretty bad because my parents, like my stepfather is a pastor and my mom is a very strong Christian. I was getting hickeys from my boyfriend and I was swearing and they thought—I wasn't doing drugs at the time—but they thought I was. Needless to say ... my home life wasn't all that great.... I kind of got forced into Christianity.

Cultural heritage for non-Aboriginal women, then, was equated with religion and sometimes class (through references to being poor and the seeming entrapment of poverty), but rarely did race, ethnicity or nationality figure into such discussions. Moreover, these women's references to cultural heritage and social positioning tended to be negative, while Aboriginal women tended to include overt and subtle references to the positive aspects of claiming a cultural Aboriginal identity. There was one notable exception to this trend among racially privileged participants. The woman, who was quoted in the earlier discussion of drug use as saying that her ability to use drugs led others to adore her, clearly recognized the advantage afforded by her cultural heritage: "I was White in a highly Native population on the street. I had blond hair at the time.... I was blond. I was White. I was sixteen. I was ... Prime."

It was not that this woman was (or claimed to be) sheltered from discrimination, exploitation or abuse, but she clearly felt—even temporarily—that her racial privilege elevated her and was clearly a source of fleeting personal satisfaction. She felt good about being White in a "highly Native population." Similarly, many of the Aboriginal women who spoke poignantly and honestly about the racism they experienced on the streets did not mean to imply that the non-Aboriginal, White youth were "privileged" in ways that allowed them to escape the exploitation or pain of the streets. Rather, these women were suggesting that, as Aboriginal girls, they were differently affected by discrimination, by racial slurs that exacerbated the verbal and physical attacks on street children, and by their difficulty fitting into society as *both* sexually abused *and* culturally marginalized. This commentary on Aboriginality and racial marginalization (and, for that matter, racial privilege) is critical to appreciate and understand because young Aboriginal women are tied to a history of colonialism that has silenced, misrepresented and completely ignored their voices. As scholars, advocates and service providers interested in assisting sexually exploited youth to improve their lives and create viable futures, we must not repeat these colonial and racist mistakes. Instead, we should try to comprehend how young Aboriginal as well as non-Aboriginal women draw on their cultural backgrounds in positive and negative ways to comprehend and counter the pain and exploitation of prostitution. As Ashley-Mika so aptly said, "I know that being Metis makes me different than the White girls even though we are made to work on the same street and take crap from the same people. Being Metis means that I get the racism that ... maybe them White girls don't. That's important, isn't it?"

Interestingly, gender does not figure prominently into these descriptions of cultural heritage. In fact, it was explicitly discussed by only a few of the research participants. However, subtler references to gender stereotypes and roles were scattered throughout the interviews. One woman, for example, mentioned that when she was a child she watched daytime television with her mother, and the highly stereotypical images of women promoted through soap operas and game shows influenced her understanding of what a woman could and should be:

> [The women have] skinny little bodies and, umm, beautiful clothes and ... lots of money.... That image of women, just even with the Barbie doll, all you see is women are sex objects. That's all I ever grew up thinking.

This woman also pointed out during her interview that the men's dorms in a lockup facility had "tougher workers" than the women's dorms had because men are more likely to challenge authority, to "abuse power" and to act out. Women are more prone, she argued, to internalize their displeasure in order to appear outwardly pleasing and compliant.

Another woman noted a similar difference in the extent to which men and women choose or are able to actively respond to their life circumstances. When recounting the ongoing abuse to which she and her brothers were subjected at the hands of their stepfather, she noted gender-based differences:

> Look at my brothers' lives. They've had their problems too but nowhere near the problems that I've had. They were able to maneuver better than I was.... My brother summed it up one time ... my pain was always internalized. Whereas men, when they're violated, when they're abused in the same way, like ... with verbal abuse and emotional abuse, their pains are more ... external. Mine was more internal, meaning it affected my soul.... The way I view myself and my relationships.

Clearly, this woman, like the one quoted before her, see women and girls as being more indelibly affected by abuse because they do not have the same room to "maneuver" that men and boys have. These assumptions correspond directly with prevailing cultural schemas of masculinity, which is imbued with assertiveness and action, and femininity, which is imbued with passivity and vulnerability.

The vulnerability ascribed to young women by the research participants was consistently seen to be exacerbated by age. The young age at which many of these women began their involvement in prostitution greatly affected how they saw themselves and found their place in the world around them. Routinely, references to "lost" childhoods, "innocent" youths and "naive" newcomers arose throughout the interviews. We found two connected but still distinct ways of describing issues of age: childhood was embraced as a marker of vulnerable and affected youth, or childhood was denied as having been irretrievably lost to dysfunctional homes and abusive streets. One woman, for example, said that from a very young age she had to be a "little adult" because the sexual exploitation to which she was exposed was a very "adult thing." Another woman repeatedly referred to her "lost childhood," and because of ongoing sexual abuse that led to her involvement in prostitution, she now believes, "I never had no childhood." Other women, however, made ready and accessible references to themselves as young and naive, often contrasting their youthful innocence against more experienced and older women (who were more likely to be referred to as "whores"):

> [In lockup remand] they treated me like a criminal there. They didn't treat me as some poor little girl who's lost her way.... They didn't care if I was, you know, some wicked evil criminal or just some poor little prostitute.

In this woman's recollection, she was a "poor little girl" and she took great exception to being treated as a criminal, an identity which she obviously reserves for those who are adults and "evil." Another woman explained that because she was a child, criminal charges against her were not pursued when she was arrested for being in a stolen car, "Yeah, I got arrested but I got off because I was so young, you know, I was twelve, what are the cops going to do?"

Motherhood: "Mother by Day, Hooker by Night."

Interestingly, most of the research participants who had children felt very strongly about the need to enrich their own children's experiences of childhood. Indeed, motherhood appeared to be a very important aspect in many of these women's lives and, for some, it was a turning point. The only time that the women participating in this study tended to clearly categorize their actions and identities was when they were discussing their children and the responsibilities of motherhood.

Approximately half of the women interviewed mentioned having children, and the vast majority of those described pregnancy and motherhood as being of great importance to them. Seeing themselves as primarily responsible for their dependent children often forced the women to compartmentalize their actions, and to some extent themselves, in order to preserve mothering and motherhood as something special and rewarding. "What do I do when I'm not working or getting high?" reflected one woman, "I love my kids." Another woman used temporal markers to define herself—"I'm a mother by day and hooker by night"—and to keep her life's activities and personal identities uncharacteristically separate. For the most part, efforts to isolate mother-hood and mothering from other aspects of themselves were more successful than when similar attempts were made in other circumstances. Despite the dangers in their lives, the vast majority of the women with children were committed to them, so much so that many women temporarily or permanently stopped working the streets and attempted to break their drug habits. The social role of motherhood gave the women a way to respect and legitimate themselves. They no longer saw themselves as "just prostitutes" (in a negative way); they could now see and represent themselves as mothers, an ideological social category that is reserved for women and certainly more revered than that of "prosti-tute."

One woman explained,

> I quit [because of] my daughter. The last three years it's been my daughter. When I was [pregnant] with her, I was clean.... She has been my big time everything. She changed everything, and that's why I quit this time, too, because I promised myself I would not do that to her. I want to see her grow up. I don't want to lose her.

Another woman explained that the fear she and a friend had of incurring a serious injury or being killed was largely related to the fact that their children would then be left alone:

> After [being beaten by a john], we didn't want to take any chances, because I have a kid and the thought of losing your kid, going out one night and not coming back and your kid's wondering, "Where's mommy?" It's enough to make you want to get off.

Echoing the commitment that these women feel toward their chil-dren, another woman spoke more generally about all children: "I believe children are the future and children should have the best, the most, the most, most of everything. Like, give them chances, numerous times if necessary." Ironically, this woman was eight months pregnant and a very frequent IV drug user. She did not address the potential difficulties that her ongoing drug use might one day cause her child, but she remained adamantly committed to the rights of children and to the importance of mothers. In her groundbreaking work on drug-using mothers, Susan Boyd (1999) claims that such contradictions are not uncommon and are often a source of great concern for women who are honestly and emotionally invested in their children but who find addictions too difficult to overcome and street communities too consuming to leave. This is certainly the case for one woman who explained,

> I swore when I got pregnant that there was no way I was ever going to give my kid a hard life and I was going to take care of him. But I was so powerless, you know, once I started drinking and doing drugs and sleeping around with all these guys again.... I remember waking up and it was one-thirty in the afternoon and I knew my kid had been up probably since nine o'clock.... And he was in his crib for five hours. And his diaper was saturated. He'd picked his diaper off of him. And I woke up, and I was so hung over. And I didn't know, like, I was a blackout drinker so I had no idea of the night before. And that scared me.

In circumstances such as these, the fear of losing their children becomes overwhelming for the women because they recognize it as a real possibility. In those cases when children were removed from the women's care, the resulting depression and despondency often exacerbated rather than countered the women's involvement in prostitution and accompanying drug use.[5] But if children are at risk, as the little boy described in the interview excerpt above might well have been, what actions can be taken? Many of the women with whom we spoke indicated that the programs that worked best for them were the ones that acknowledged the importance of motherhood and did not require the women to leave their children in order to pursue counselling or treatment. One woman found an exit program to be particularly useful because the workers engaged with her children, played with them and made her feel special because she was their mother. Seeking assistance through this program was a positive experience for both the woman and her children. Another young woman indicated that her involvement in prostitution was largely to support her children, and if adequate social services and financial resources were available, she would have quit eagerly, long before she ultimately did. Being aware that financial desperation sometimes plays a major role in the women's decision to continue their involvement in prostitution is critically important when considering how services and programs could be combined to provide the necessities for life. This is not an easy task, as service providers are well aware, but our research strongly suggests that the rewards are more than worth it: "Now I know I'm not one of those people any more. I have children and I want to take care of them."

Conclusion

In my last meeting with Ashley-Mika, she said,

> Like, I started this when I was, like, twelve or whatever. I had no clue who the hell I was but there were important things that made me feel like a good person or bad person. I still, like, don't know for sure who or what I am now, but I'd like to find out.

As we work towards offering relief to sexually exploited youth, we must think carefully about how the youth see themselves and how they construct self-identities, social networks and feelings of belonging. We cannot rely on preconceived assumptions or singular accounts of exploitation; for our response to have meaning for the young women themselves, we must instead explore how influencing factors come together to shape their lives, self-regard and communities. We must explore how they use whatever resources they can, not only to explain and justify their lives to themselves and others, but also to change and alter the course of their lives.

Notes

1. Ashley-Mika is a pseudonym chosen by the participant. The process by which she chose this name reveals a great deal about how she constructs a complex self-identity as a Metis woman involved in prostitution. For further discussion see Downe (2001). The other women with whom we spoke are referred to as research participants.
2. "Escort girls" refers to young women who were associated, in one way or another, with established escort service agencies.
3. The phrase "systems of prostitution" is used here to refer to the various degrees of institutionalization that characterize the sale of sex for money or consideration. This term encompasses the following: transnational and highly organized sex trafficking; locally known and well-established prostitute and pimp networks that are located in escort agencies, massage parlours, on the streets and other sites; as well as more spontaneous and less predictable forms of prostitution. These various "systems" often operate according to different rules and patterns but there are commonalities. The exploitation of children and youth occurs within all these systems.
4. "Grabbing" here refers to selling sex.
5. For a very good discussion of how the loss of children can exacerbate drug abuse, see Campbell (2000).

Chapter Three

"That Was My Prayer Every Night— Just to Get Home Safe"
Violence in the Lives of Girls Exploited Through Prostitution

Kendra Nixon and Leslie M. Tutty

> It's just too bad that life involves so much abuse and violence. Everywhere you get it, the police, everywhere. You get battered around, even if it's just with words. It gets to you. It gets to your spirit and you start feeling like you don't want to be around anymore.

Even though the sexual exploitation of children through prostitution is a serious problem in Canada, the impact of violence on girls while on the street has rarely been examined. This chapter documents the violence experienced by forty-seven women from across the Prairie provinces who had become involved in prostitution prior to age eighteen. Although we did not ask specific questions about abuse and violence in our interviews, information about it emerged in response to queries such as "How did you become involved in prostitution?" and "What services and resources did you find helpful?" The extent to which violence and abuse emerged in the women's narratives was startling. In addition to documenting the many facets of violence endured by the participants, we also identify strategies that the women used for protection and suggest implications for policy, practice and prevention.

Violence: The Everyday Occurrence

We know that girls exploited through prostitution experience considerable violence in their lives, both while living with their families of origin and during their involvement in prostitution. While we consider that the act of engaging in sex work is abusive in and of itself, research shows that those on the street experience multiple victimizations. Violence must be conceptualized broadly (Berman and Jiwani 2002). In addition to sexual and physical victimization, the women with whom we spoke had experienced numerous and varying manifestations of violence including verbal and psychological abuse, racism, classism and poverty. All of these forms of oppression serve as mechanisms to control or dominate women involved in sex work. Regardless of the form that violence takes, it ultimately undermines a woman's sense of self and reinforces her powerlessness (Alliance of Five Research Centres on Violence 1999). This chapter details the experiences of street-involved women using their own words to provide a personal sense of the profound impact of the violence.

Childhood Victimization

We asked how the women first became exploited by prostitution as girls or adolescents. According to previous research, a history of childhood abuse is common. For example, in Canadian research by Benoit and Millar (2001) almost 90 percent of the study participants reported a history of some physical, sexual or emotional abuse (see also Bagley and Young 1987; Farley and Barkan 1998; Gemme et al. 1984; Lowman 2000; McIntyre 1999; Nadon et al. 1998; Pyett and Warr 1999).

It is generally agreed that Canadian youth exploited through prostitution have a higher than expected history of childhood sexual abuse. In McIntyre's (1999) study, 82 percent of the youth had been sexually abused prior to their involvement in prostitution compared to 20 to 30 percent of children in the general population (Badgley 1984). Similarly, a Montreal study conducted by Gemme and colleagues (1984) reported that 45 percent had been victims of incest before becoming involved in prostitution. Bagley and Young (1987) also noted high levels of childhood sexual abuse.

While some have proposed a direct connection between childhood sexual abuse and entry into prostitution, others suggest that sexual abuse should not be considered a cause of prostitution involvement (Brannigan and Van Brunschot 1997; Mathews 1989). Rather, the intersection of abusive experiences within the family, running away, a lack of viable alternatives and the failure of the child welfare system cumulatively create a situation that sets the stage for children to become involved in prostitution (Chesney-Lind and Shelden 1992; Mathews 1989; Schissel and Fedec 1999). Others have argued that the level of sexual abuse among exploited youth is no different from that in the general population (Brannigan and Fleischman 1989).

There also appears to be a high proportion of childhood physical abuse in this population. In the 1998 Canadian study by Nadon and colleagues, 48 percent of the respondents had been physically abused as children. Further,, Bagley and Young (1987) noted that 60 to 70 percent of their research participants involved in prostitution had a physical abuse history.

While we did not explicitly ask most of the women about past or current victimization, they disclosed rates of childhood sexual abuse consistent with those previously reported. Five women specified that they had not been abused in their families; however, most of the others had a history of childhood abuse. The abuse was primarily sexual, with two children experiencing physical abuse and one, severe neglect. Fathers or stepfathers, and other male adults such as mothers' boyfriends were the most likely to sexually abuse the young girls.

Some girls were repeatedly victimized. One woman commented that, "I'd been molested all my life." In answer to the question "What was your family life like at the time you began working?" another replied, "Very dysfunctional. I was sexually abused at a very early age. I was raped over and over again." A third woman disclosed, "I was sexually abused as a child. I come from a normal home. My parents never drank, never did drugs, never abused us. I was sexually abused by uncles, and I had no idea why child welfare took me from my parents, and that's where it all started."

Several of the women had been raped by peers when young:

> I got raped when I was about eleven by one of my really good guy friends and after that, I felt like crap about myself. It just went down hill from there. I made choices based on how I was feeling. [Really self-destructive kind of stuff?] Yeah, I'm still good at that.

> After the grade eight dance, I tagged up with some people I didn't know that well. Ended up getting really drunk and that's the night I lost my virginity.... I was gang-raped. At the time I didn't see it as being gang-raped because I thought, "Oh I was drunk." Some of the guys I knew, but it was just a whole bunch of people from the different high schools. I remember two details: having four or five guys around me and then I was moved to a bedroom and it was just a gang rape.

Several women considered their involvement in prostitution as one way to control and overcome the feelings of powerlessness that stemmed from their childhood abuse. One commented, "When you're sexually abused, I always thought I had control over the men. I never thought about it as they're using me. I always thought I had the power. The more money I made, the more wanted and loved I felt because I always associated love with sex." Another woman admitted that after having been paid by her uncle to perform numerous sexual acts, "No customer after that really seemed to matter. It never really made a difference. I just made sure that I got paid."

Victimization While Involved in Prostitution as Children and Youth

Canadian researchers have reported that adult women often experience severe violence while involved in prostitution (Benoit and Millar 2001; Lowman 2000; Lowman and Fraser 1995). In Benoit and Millar's 2001 study, almost all of the adult women involved in their research had experienced at least one violent incident. In Canada from 1992 to 1998, Lowman (2000) noted that at least eighty-six women had been murdered while involved in street prostitution. Further, at the time that this chapter was written, sixty-seven women (all presumed to have been involved in prostitution) have disappeared from Vancouver's Eastside. A suspect, charged with murdering fifteen of these women, is currently on trial.

While childhood abuse and violence against adult women involved in prostitution have been well documented, less has been written about the experiences of street youth or the impact of violence on their decisions to seek out and use services that could ultimately support their exit from prostitution and protect them from further abuse. In a study of homeless youth in Seattle, Tyler, Whitbeck, Hoyt and Cauce. (2001: 452) concluded that homeless youth who engage in sex-trade work for survival are vulnerable to further sexual victimization because they are highly visible and accessible. Moreover, there has been relatively little focus on violence by pimps and customers against children involved in prostitution. In 1992, the National Center for Missing and Exploited Children in the United States reported that exploited youth are often assaulted by pimps to ensure their obedience and prevent them from leaving. Children may also fear retaliation by pimps who have threatened to hurt them or their families if they leave (Assistant Deputy Ministers' Committee on Prostitution and the Sexual Exploitation of Youth 2000).

Almost all of the women that we interviewed reported extreme violence when involved in prostitution. Many had friends or acquaintances that had been murdered while prostituting.

> I've come close to dying a few times.

> You get raped, you get beat, you get killed. I lost my partner because of the streets.

> I figure I probably should have been dead at least ten times.

The women perceived the violence as normal or to be expected.

> I have seen girls thrown into fences, licks from their boyfriends.... I have grown to think that it's common. We see that down here all the time.

> If something bad happened, I wouldn't have known the difference. That to me would have just been normal.

> I've only had four bad dates in my whole life. That says a lot, I think. I'm very careful when I go out there because I don't want to kill myself.

A number of women described becoming numb or desensitized to the violence. Such reactions can be considered as coping mechanisms to deal with the emotional responses associated with having been traumatized. However, trauma reactions also keep young women involved in prostitution by leading them to ignore or suppress their own emotional distress.

> A police officer showed me picture after picture of dead girls, and I still worked for eight years after that. You're numb to that after a while.

> I've had plenty of bad dates. I probably should have quit before I saw the things I've seen. I was only out there for two and a half years, off and on, but you get to know people and you see things, and you become cold inside. It just doesn't faze you anymore.

Violence from Pimps and Intimate Partners

Half of the women reported violence or threats of violence from pimps while involved in prostitution. Since not all of the women were asked about violence from pimps this number likely underestimates how often it occurs. Interestingly, only one participant claimed that she had never been threatened or assaulted by her pimp. Although female friends or acquaintances introduced the majority of the women interviewed to prostitution, nine were forced, coerced or intimidated into prostitution by pimps or abusive intimate partners.

> I was introduced to it because I was drugged up. Then I was put out.

> I was thirteen. I had a gun held to my head. I wasn't sure if it was loaded or not, but at the time I was pretty scared. And they told me that if I went to cops or told my group home staff that they, when they got out or they'll get someone to kill me. So I was pretty scared.

> I fell into his game and he addicted me to crack cocaine and put me out on the street to pay for my habit later on.

Once involved, a number were severely beaten if they refused to prostitute themselves. One young woman commented, "They came to me and said, 'We want you to make five hundred bucks in two hours.' I said that was impossible and so they took my arm and broke it."

Other women were frightened to leave prostitution because their pimps might retaliate. This, not surprisingly, represented a major barrier to exiting. One woman commented that, "He threatened us [that] if we ever left, he'd show us big rifles. He had other men with him, so if you tried to escape, his other buddies would go looking for us." Another woman noted, "I've always thought if I could [leave] safely, I would." As a third woman reflected, "If you want to break free, it's hard. They don't want you to leave because you're making money for them."

Frequently, women were afraid to access services because they would be punished if their pimps found out. These pimps were controlling, constantly watching the women.

> The pimp I was with at the time was very controlling. It [accessing services] would have been dreadful for me. It didn't matter where you went, in any big city, there was a family member there, so there was nowhere to hide to talk to someone.

> I was out there at a certain time, back in, didn't talk to anybody. I was being pimped. I was told to go out and get so much money and make sure I stayed where I was supposed to. They were always watching me and I don't know what would happen if I had talked to someone. They were always just across the street from me.

Twenty-two women reported having been physically, sexually, verbally and financially abused by their intimate partners. Eleven had been coerced into prostituting by men that they identified as boyfriends rather than as pimps.

> I just got sick of the abuse and I'd be getting a punch in the face and [he] told me not to do anything to piss him off that day and he went out and told me to go to work.

> He [boyfriend] was beating me ... just punching me in the face and everything ... standing at the corner, my eyes were just black and he made me stand there. Like I couldn't get picked up. He said I have to stand there ... he was going to beat the shit out of me right there.

The abuse and exploitation that the women experienced from those that they considered intimate partners closely resembles the controlling tactics used by pimps. For example, both use brutal tactics such as physical and sexual violence, threats and intimidation, financial exploitation, and isolation, to ensure women's compliance. Interestingly, the women rarely referred to their intimate partners as pimps.

Violence from Customers

More than half of the women reported experiencing violence, also known as "bad dates," from customers or "johns." This proportion is likely an underestimate, since not all of the women were explicitly asked about such violence. Only three women claimed to have never had a bad date. McIntyre (1999) reported that, in reflecting on their experiences as exploited youth, 82 percent of her study participants had experienced "bad dates."

Most of the women we interviewed described numerous incidences of violent acts perpetrated by customers. One woman commented, "I had a lot of bad dates. I got raped quite a few times. I've got beaten up quite a few times." Another succinctly stated, "I've had bad dates like crazy." Finally, another mentioned, "I've been hit by a car. I've been raped at gun point."

The assaults included being stabbed or cut, raped, gang-raped, raped at gun point, forced to engage in degrading sexual acts, choked/strangled, beaten, kidnapped, stalked, gun held to head, tied up, tortured, beaten with objects such as baseball bats or crowbars, and run over. These incidents often resulted in hospitalization and serious injuries such as miscarriages, stitches, paralysis, broken bones and fractures. One woman described how, "The guy who I had a bad date with is in jail for fifteen years. He cut me from asshole to belly button. I had stitches from here to there and everywhere." Another narrated, "I ended up in the hospital one time for three days. He [customer] took a crowbar and whipped me all over the head and my legs. I couldn't even open my eyes … [he] broke my nose."

The women also categorized being robbed, having men refuse to pay after sex or being left stranded outside the city as "bad dates." One woman offered, "Some of 'em would just get off on me for nothing and then refuse to pay, you know. I hate that."

Several women commented that they constantly feared bad dates and not knowing if they would come back alive. This fear was pervasive and ongoing. They commented that, "You never know who you are going to jump in with or if you were going to come home. You didn't know if you're going to get beat up or if you're going to make any money." Another mentioned, "You're always thinking about the bad

dates or the rapes or whatever. I have a real hard time shaking that off."
A third women summed up, "The uncertainty of it ... just a feeling of
being vulnerable."

Not surprisingly numerous women commented that they needed to
be intoxicated or high while prostituting because their fear was so
overwhelming.

> I was on speed and that drug really makes you feel invincible. I would not die.
> I wasn't scared of anything. I wasn't scared of anybody, so [fear of bad dates]
> wasn't an issue.

> At first for me it was kind of scary and I needed to drink to bring out the
> courage in me to go out there.

> I used to go on the street but I had to have a drink or smoke up. I'd be right
> out there. I wouldn't be scared of nothing.

The violence that the women experienced both in childhood and during
their involvement in prostitution was associated with many reporting
such low self-esteem and internalized self-hatred that they stopped
caring about themselves. Thus, they continued working on the street.

> The dangers of living out on the street never got to me. I was never afraid
> because I don't I think I cared if something ever happened to me. I really did
> not care.

> After a while of being abused, you stop caring and you stop caring about your
> body. Sometimes you just don't care if you're safe or not.

One third of the women were abused not only by pimps, customers
and intimate partners, but also by other women involved in prostitution.
This violence included physical assaults, being threatened, robbed or
forced "off stroll." One woman described her experience: "When I was
younger I was working, this one girl was jealous of me. [I] got my ass
beaten. They all jumped in and I ended up getting kicked like almost
twelve times right with a steel-toed boot. I had a crack in my bone, my
cheek bone."

Several women acknowledged that their pimps protected them
against violence from other women and their pimps. One young woman
admitted, "If you don't have a pimp and you try to stand around there,
you'll get beaten up ... the girls attacked a girl."

Violence from Police and Other Professionals

Women also reported violence from service providers, most commonly the police. Although a number of women had good relationships or were neutral about the police, about one fifth (nine women) had been assaulted, sexually assaulted or propositioned by police officers. As one woman noted, "I've been raped by a police officer.... I don't trust them." Another described:

> I got arrested and the police grabbed me, they banged my head on the paddy wagon. They dragged me behind the police station downtown, dragged me on the gravel. My whole face was swollen, I had scratches all down my legs.... They beat me up real bad.

Six of the nine women who had experienced violence from the police were of Aboriginal origin. This high proportion may be due to their relative lack of power and credibility because of their racial backgrounds, or may indicate racism on the part of some police officers. While nine women reporting such abusive treatment is a relatively small number, the fact that six were Aboriginal is cause for concern.

Other women reported that the police harassed and verbally assaulted them. As one woman commented:

> [Police] pick on you—"What's your name? What do you do? Why are you out here? You don't have I.D. so screw off. You're not allowed back on the stroll." Some cops are really ignorant and rude. If you're on the stroll they look at you like you're lower than them. They're above the law. They can do whatever they want. Some cops come up to you say, "I'm gonna stick you in jail for seventy-two hours just because I can!"

Several women feared the police, based either on their own negative experiences or having listened to others:

> We were running from the police. We were scared of them. Nothing ever happened to me, but you hear all kinds of things where police would be totally abusing their power. I don't know if they'd actually go ahead and have sex with workers but they'd be touching them and what not, like touching them and not arresting them.

Not surprisingly, a number of women commented that they would not seek help from the police, fearing criminal charges, arrest or being assaulted. As one young woman commented, "If you have a bad date on the street, the cops won't offer you much. They'll jack you up and haul your ass down to the police station." Another stated, "I don't trust them.... I was so scared. Nothing that [would] put me in touch with the cops—I wouldn't have used nothing like that." A third woman mentioned, "I don't trust them. It's not gonna be much help if you try to get safe only to have some fucking cop getting off on you."

Almost two thirds of the women had been involved with the child welfare system when very young. Of these, most were taken into care and resided in foster and group homes, often for many years. Three reported having been either physically or sexually abused by caretakers while residing in these out-of-home placements. One respondent commented, "He [a group home staff] did pay me for sex. He did tell me later that, like a threat, 'You better never tell anybody about this.' He still works."

Professionals working in other institutions sexually assaulted two additional women as children. As one woman recalled, "One of the teachers raped me a few months before I went there. The system is trying to protect me, yet they put me in a place where a rapist was. That's why it's hard for me to trust any government organizations."

Violence from Members of the Public

The women also experienced violence from the mainstream or "straight" culture when they were involved in prostitution. Having eggs or pennies thrown at them by passers-by, being called derogatory names, or being groped, caused several women to feel demeaned. In addition to the violence experienced while working, fellow students harassed several women when they returned to schools after they had left the streets. One young woman commented, "I heard some girls call me a whore and I just lost it. I ended up fighting with one of the girls and the teacher found us and, of course, I got hauled off to the principal's office."

Several women described feeling judged by the public: "[The general public] see that you're low." And, "I couldn't go out. If I go to the store, they look at me and say, 'Oh, you're a hooker.'" Another mentioned that, "Everybody is watching you and knowing that you're a whore."

The fear of being judged prevented many women from accessing services. As one woman commented, "I didn't want nobody's help. They were going to turn me down anyway or look at me as if I was dirty."

Violence Against Others and Self-Directed Abuse

Seventeen women disclosed that they were physically violent to others such as intimate partners, other women involved in prostitution, customers, group home staff and police. Five admitted having a criminal record for serious assaults or weapons offences. Some attributed their own aggressive behaviour to drug use or becoming hardened by their time on the street.

> Even with the solvents ... I get very aggressive when I'm on that stuff. I want to fight everybody around me.

> My anger and abusiveness became a real problem. Some women will take abuse for the rest of their life. I went the total opposite. I became very angry. I tried to kill a guy.

However, although a number were violent towards others, they more often directed their violence internally, reporting self-harm, self-mutilation and cutting, and thoughts of suicide.

> When I'm in pain I like to hurt myself because the pain goes away.

> Slashing makes me not think about who is hurting me and I would rather hurt myself than let people hurt me. If someone was hurting me at the time, I would cut myself.

> After you're raped you can't function. Especially getting raped twice within a month. It was too much for me. I think if I was ever really close to actually killing myself that would have been it.

Seven mentioned that they had attempted suicide; three reported multiple attempts. One woman commented about her own thoughts of suicide:

> Just before my eighteenth birthday I tried to kill myself because I did not want to be responsible for who I was as an adult, you know. I never looked into the future. I still have problems thinking about where I'm gonna be in six months. There was no future. It was day by day by day.

One woman commented, "It's like being an abused wife, I guess. After a while, you think that there's nothing else you can do, that nobody else wants you."

Protective Strategies

The women were not simply victims, but were often resourceful and resilient. In the face of pervasive violence, most adopted protective strategies to keep themselves safe from violent customers. Women involved in prostitution do not see traditional means of ensuring personal safety, such as requesting assistance from the police, as options. Rather, they rely on themselves and a system of "street smarts." These strategies included carrying weapons, remaining sober while with customers, paying attention to their "instincts," having other women watch or accompany them when with customers and following "the rules" of the street.

Rarely did women leave prostitution in response to violent experiences. Instead, these incidents motivated them to adopt strategies to deal with the expected violence that comes with their work. Securing control of possibly dangerous situations became critical. For example, eight women remained sober while working to protect themselves and ensure that they could escape if they felt threatened. As one told us, "I think I'm more aware of what's going on when I'm straight." Another mentioned that, "I'd rather be able to get out of the situation than fall over because I'm too drunk or stoned." A third woman described it as, "more of a fear thing. If I was high, it would take me a lot more time to figure what the hell was going on if I was having a bad date."

Some women spoke about being good judges of people and using their instincts to discern whether a customer might turn violent.

> I don't recall ever having a bad date when I've been sober. Because I can read people very well and if I don't like the way I feel … I don't need the money that bad to get high. [I'd] say, "sorry, buddy let me out of here."

> I trust my instincts. That's the only main weapon I have out there. I trust them and so far I haven't really had a bad date.

> It's a feeling. You got to have them feelings if you're on the street. If you don't got them, you die.

Following the "rules" was another protective strategy that women used to keep themselves safe from violent customers.

> I followed the rules. There was no vans, not more than one person. I did not go out of the downtown area.

> I wouldn't go with young guys or big, muscular people. I'd go with older guys. If a young guy was too quick to say yes to a price, I'd be like, "take a hike." He's going to try and beat me up or give me the money and then after, take it back or whatever.

> I'd say, "come to my place or not at all." If it's in the car, it's got to be where I go. I don't ever go to their spots.

> I won't go with you if you're drinking, if you're stoned, if your car has garbage all over.

The women often stayed in pairs or groups or they carried weapons to keep themselves safe from bad dates. One described how, "We wouldn't leave each other. We'd take each other's [licence] plates." Another commented that, "Two girls would always stand with me and they would tell them that I wouldn't do lays. I only do hand jobs and blow jobs." Yet a third noted that, "[Stiletto heels] were my weapon and my keys. I always have keys in my hand. They're a great weapon." As a final woman succinctly stated, "I was raped once but then I carried a knife, so I didn't have too much of a problem after that."

Summing Up

Barnard (1993) has noted a tendency to think of sexually transmitted diseases, such as HIV infection and STD transmission, as the major risk associated with prostitution. Although such health issues are serious concerns, the risk of injury and death from violent assaults is considerable, as is indicated by the accounts of the women here. Violence and abuse were dominant themes in the women's narratives.

In summary, while we did not explicitly ask most of the women about historical or current victimization, they disclosed rates of childhood sexual abuse consistent with those reported by other Canadian researchers. The violence and abuse continued after the girls became involved in prostitution, similar to previous research examining violence and prostitution. The women reported abuse from pimps, customers, intimate partners, other women involved in prostitution, police, group home staff and the general public. The violence was often serious, frequently resulting in painful and life-threatening injuries. Although violence from pimps or customers prompted many to contemplate leaving prostitution, few actually did. The women viewed violence by pimps and "bad dates" as normal and even an expected "part of the job." Several women expressed relief that they only had "two or three" bad dates. Their readiness to accept violence in sex work has previously been noted by Pyett and Warr, who found that "street workers were prepared to accept violence as a condition of working in an illegal and socially marginalized occupation" (1999: 194).

A number of the women lived with daily fear that profoundly affected their self-image and, ultimately, their ability to seek and obtain assistance from various helping professionals. Similar to woman abuse by intimate partners, the participants admitted that violence was a significant and real barrier to leaving their environment. They were often controlled by pimps or abusive boyfriends, and feared the consequences of attempting to leave or accessing services.

The women spoke of violence and threats of violence from other women involved in prostitution; some depended on their pimps to protect them. Helping professionals victimized others. Other children in care in the Canadian child welfare system have reported similar experiences (Raychaba 1993). A number of women chose not to access services because they were fearful and did not trust those in positions of authority, especially the police. The women were also physically and verbally harassed by members of the general public, resulting in shame and humiliation.

The women described the effects of the violence not only in terms of physical injuries but also of the tremendous emotional toll. Self-destructive, self-injurious behaviours and suicidal thoughts are common trauma reactions. Self-harm is a necessary, albeit unhealthy, way of responding to emotionally distressing and oppressive conditions stemming from traumatic childhood and adult experiences (Fillmore, Dell and the Elizabeth Fry Society of Manitoba 2000). Several women saw the violence in their lives as causing their own aggressive behaviours towards others, as they became "hardened" by the dangerous street life.

Implications for Policy and Practice

The women's experiences highlight the importance of creating strategies to address violence against girls and young women exploited through prostitution. Successful programs will likely utilize different strategies from those in adult services and will also use non-traditional service delivery modes. The women described numerous barriers to connecting with services including fear of retaliation by pimps and their own fears of about being judged and stigmatized by mainstream helping professionals. Early intervention with street-involved young girls is a crucial strategy in preventing the levels of violence and the serious negative effects described by the women we interviewed.

Reactions such as numbing, desensitization and avoidance are considered by some as coping mechanisms to deal with the emotional reactions associated with having been traumatized. A trauma perspective could be adopted by service agencies to assist in understanding the profound impact of the multiple acts of violence on these girls' lives and how the perpetuating cycle of abuse often keeps young women entrenched in street prostitution. The women described to us the experience of becoming numb or desensitized to the violence: these are key features of Post-traumatic Stress Syndrome (PTSD) (van der Kolk, McFarlane and Weisaeth 1996). The trauma literature on childhood sexual abuse has long noted the tendency for some child survivors to act out by behaving in overtly sexualized and provocative ways. Rape trauma (Foa et al. 1991) and trauma in reaction to abuse by intimate partners (Tutty 1998) have also been identified as mechanisms that not only create unpleasant reactions in victims, but interfere with counselling and problem-solving techniques that might address the abuse. Almost all of the women with whom we spoke experienced one or all of these forms of violence.

Several researchers in the field of victimization also use trauma terminology to describe the emotional symptoms of a number of women exploited through prostitution (Farley, Baral, Kiremire and Sezgin 1998; Farley and Barkan 1998). In Farley and colleagues' 1998 comparison of PTSD symptomatology across five countries, women involved in prostitution had similarly high levels of such symptoms. Trauma reactions also keep young women involved in prostitution by causing them to ignore or suppress their own emotional distress. While utilizing a trauma perspective has been criticized as pathologizing women by applying psychiatric terminology and diagnosis, it acknowledges that reactions such as numbing or hypervigilance stem from normal reactions to traumatic events rather than any inherent problem in the individual. In essence, if any of us were in a similar situation, we would likely respond in the same manner. Further, it explains the multiple victimization experiences in a way that does not blame the victim. Understanding numbing, avoidance and hypervigilance as possible trauma reactions could change the manner in which helping professionals connect with and offer services to these young women.

Many, if not all, of the women reported that their involvement in prostitution—either starting or returning to prostitution was directly related to economic security. A number began their involvement as a way to survive on the street. As children, they had no other means of meeting their basic needs. Programs and policies that aim to assist girls to exit prostitution must take into account the poverty in which they live and understand that their involvement in prostitution is truly about "survival sex."

Looking at the girls' and young women's interaction with the youth protection and social service systems, it becomes apparent why they would be reluctant to access traditional services. The majority had first been abused in some way by family members, then removed and placed into alternative living arrangements such as foster care or group homes: in these facilities they were then abused by their caregivers. Further, while those in the general public generally consider the police to be the most obvious source of help if one has been assaulted, few of the women we interviewed saw the police as a resource. This may be especially true for Aboriginal women. Several had been sexually abused, propositioned, harassed and physically assaulted by the police, or they knew of colleagues who had received such treatment. It should not be surprising that their previous negative experiences with the very systems that should have protected them left many reluctant to trust social and health services.

The social service system has responded well to the challenge of helping abused women who choose to return to abusive partners a number of times, before they successfully leave permanently. These patterns are similar to the process of children and youth moving in and out of prostitution. It raises the question of whether services to women and children involved in prostitution should not be conceptualized in a similar manner to services provided for battered women. Although the programs would need to be specialized, the goal is the same—the prevention of violence and abuse against women and children. The culture of services for battered women has much to teach us about respecting the rights and autonomy of survivors while promoting protection and safety. The history of services for battered women has also taught us how critical the provision of secure funding is to support the often lengthy process of disengaging from abusive relationships. Finally, both programs could benefit from an exchange of ideas and program models between shelter workers and street workers.

Recently, in Western Canada, programs to prevent the sexual exploitation of children have been developed and marketed to school systems, primarily at the high school level. Such a primary prevention focus may be misguided, given the high proportion of women in the current study who started prostituting before the age of fifteen. Prostitution prevention programs that challenge the myth of a glamorous life in prostitution (as is portrayed in the movie, *Pretty Woman*) may change the attitudes of both young men and women towards those exploited through prostitution. However, the majority of that audience is likely beyond the age at which they are vulnerable to the lure of the street life.

Rather, a secondary prevention approach targeting the "at-risk" young adolescents in foster care and group homes would be more appropriate. Further, a tertiary prevention approach of providing treatment to children who have been sexually abused could address the serious long-term effects of such abuse and prevent the development of trauma symptoms that may predispose the youth to get involved on the streets. Such treatment is considerably less available than in the past, given current governmental budgetary constraints. As well, the general public is now much less likely to see sexual abuse as the serious issue it was considered to be in the 1980s and early 1990s: a scepticism about its prevalence and importance has developed in recent years.

Conclusion

As documented by the women in our study, the violence that they experienced when involved in street prostitution as young women was common and serious. Not only are such girls likely to have histories of childhood sexual and physical victimization, but they also experience extreme and pervasive violence on the street, frequently resulting in painful and life-threatening injuries. Almost everyone with whom they were in contact, not only pimps, customers and other women involved in prostitution, but also the police and professionals who should have been acting as protectors rather than perpetrators abused the women. Although violence from pimps or johns prompted many to contemplate leaving prostitution, few actually did, even perceiving such abuse as a normal "part of the job." While others have documented the extent of the violence experienced by girls who are sexually exploited through prostitution, understanding its everyday context and pervasive nature is critical when developing services and strategies to assist girls and adolescents to contemplate exiting.

Chapter Four

"I Don't Know What the Hell It Is But It Sounds Nasty"

Health Issues for Girls Working the Streets

Pamela J. Downe

Introduction

For at least one hundred years, concerns about the effects of prostitution have been consistently couched in terms of health and well-being, in part because the concern lies more with clients and the ubiquitous "general public" than with those who are sexually exploited through prostitution. These concerns have intensified in the last two decades as the HIV/AIDS pandemic has escalated and the risks for those exploited through systems of prostitution have become increasingly recognized (see Farmer 1999). However, little is known about how street-involved youth actually experience, assess, prioritize and respond to health-threatening conditions. Nor is much known about how service providers facilitate health-seeking behaviours among clients affected by prostitution. Cecilia Benoit and Alison Millar's (2001) recent report on the working conditions, health status and exiting experiences of young women and men involved in systems of prostitution[1] in British Columbia is a laudable step in that direction, as are several other key works (e.g., Brussa 1998; Downe 1997; Raymond 2001). Much still needs to be done, however, in order to fully appreciate what "health" means to sexually exploited youth and how they experience the risks and ramifications of their street involvement.

The purpose of this chapter is to present the health-related information that emerged from our interviews with the fifty-seven participating women who were, as youth, exploited through prostitution.[2] Health is a paramount concern for those exploited through prostitution as well as for those offering services to them. Health-related conditions are actually experienced and understood in more integrated ways, so that one issue overlaps with at least one other. Therefore, while this study cannot speak to the actual health status of sexually exploited youth in a medical way, it can provide important insights into how young women integrate health-related conditions into their experiences on the streets and at other sites of prostitution.

"The Fifty Odd Things That Are Out There": Making Links Among HIV/AIDS, Sexually Transmitted Infections, Drugs and Violence

Sexual health, with a strong emphasis on HIV/AIDS, is the primary focus of most health-related studies of prostitution and sexual exploitation. This is not surprising given that the HIV/AIDS epidemic among youth has received considerable and ongoing media attention. Health Canada (2002) notes that, although youth currently constitute only a small proportion (less than 4 percent) of the total HIV and AIDS cases in Canada, a recent United Nations AIDS (2001) report indicates that an estimated 10.3 million youth (between the ages of fifteen and twenty-four years) are living with HIV/AIDS worldwide. Moreover, the world's youth now account for almost half of all the new cases of HIV and AIDS reported globally (UNAIDS 2001). In Canada, street youth have much higher rates of HIV/AIDS infection than youth who are not street-involved. A study in Vancouver, for example, found that, during the period 1996–2001, the prevalence rate of HIV among drug-injecting youth was 17 percent, and that, because of restricted economic re-sources, greater vulnerability to violence and a higher rate of involve-ment in prostitution, young women were more likely to be infected than were young men (Miller et al. 2002).[3] It is important to emphasize that the risk of infection faced by street-involved girls is mostly related to their unprotected sex with boyfriends, sharing contaminated needles and vulnerability to sexual assault, rather than being connected to their specific involvement in prostitution (Epele 2002). However, these sources of HIV/AIDS risk are often eclipsed in public health and media reports by a presiding focus on prostitution. In fact, even though women and girls were largely excluded from technical and popular representations of the epidemic in its first few years when the risks to the "general public" were still relatively unknown, "prostitutes"—the majority of whom were recognized to be female—were identified fairly early on by politically influential centres for health research (like the centres for disease control) as being a potential "risk group" and "reservoir" for the virus (Guinan and Hardy 1987; Treichler 1988). There has, therefore, been a fairly consistent equation between prostitution and HIV/AIDS.

Given all this, it is not surprising that over half (twenty-two) of the forty participants who discussed health issues mentioned HIV/AIDS, though none reported having contracted it. HIV/AIDS was frequently recognized by the women with whom we spoke as a prevailing threat. One woman (an IV drug user) echoed the sentiments of several others when she said that she felt "lucky" not to have it:

> I'm still lucky not to have like Hepatitis C or AIDS or anything like that, [my] insides aren't messed up obviously. I've been able to have children. Like it's, it's not been that way for some reason.

Another woman was particularly concerned about contracting the infection because she had closely witnessed the difficulties associated with it when she watched her mother die of HIV/AIDS-related causes. She explained that she did not want to end up like her mother; her memories of finding out about her mother's illness were quite vivid:

> [My mom] had AIDS ever since I was about seven but she didn't tell anybody.... I was the first one to find out and then I'm the one that had to tell the whole family 'cause everybody thought it was cancer. It wasn't cancer, it was AIDS. And I didn't believe her so she took me to the clinic and I talked to some guy [who] ... explained to me that "your mom got raped in 1984" ... and that's how she contracted AIDS.

This young woman was put into a foster home and, after her mother's death, wanted to "get on with life" but the stigma of HIV/AIDS in the late 1980s made it very difficult for her:

> After my mom died, I just wanted to go on with my life and it took me five schools to graduate because my mom went on [the] news when I was fourteen to tell everybody she had AIDS. And then I went to this school, that school— "Oh, wasn't her mom, like, on the news saying she had AIDS? Like, how do we know she doesn't have AIDS?" You know, soon as I heard that, I just, I just packed up and left. I couldn't handle that.

It is relevant to note here that in moving from one school to the next, as well as from one foster home to another without adequate social support, this young woman began her involvement in prostitution as a way to secure some financial independence and gain a sense of belonging. However, she remained acutely mindful of the realities of HIV/AIDS, particularly those associated with sexual aggression and assault. Indeed, all her references to her mother's death, to HIV/AIDS more generally and to the prevailing health risks of prostitution are incorporated in one way or another in discussions of sexual aggression, abuse and the need for safe places where protection can be offered.

Associating HIV/AIDS with the violence so commonly encountered by those involved in prostitution was not rare. Seventeen women (77 percent of those making reference to HIV/AIDS and almost 40 percent of the total) made this link. When asked about the most serious kinds of health problems faced by exploited youth, for example, one woman did not hesitate to indicate that "violence" stood out as a particular threat but she quickly associated it with other health-related conditions. While the women did not assert that it is possible to contract HIV/AIDS from violent assaults, they did offer experience-based knowledge that supports the mounting medical literature showing definitively that violence is an exacerbating factor which operates by reducing immunity and increasing susceptibility. When asked what constituted the most pressing health problem faced by youth exploited through prostitution, one woman explained:

> Violence. And, like, with, just with some of the men out there. Um, um, definitely like AIDS, STDs, Hepatitis C with, with sharing needles. It's all part of the life. It's like, you know, I, I think about it and I think I was so careful with condoms and stuff, um, until the first time I was raped.

It is interesting that the initial reference to violence spilled quickly into a discussion of specific infections, drug use and then back to sexualized violence. Clearly, all these conditions overlap, becoming intertwined into one burden of illness and risk that is considered to be just "part of the life."

The connection between HIV/AIDS and other sexually transmitted infections, such as that made in the interview excerpt above, was also quite common. One woman, for example, said that the most pressing health concerns for those involved in prostitution were "HIV, hep-C and, you know, many of the other fifty-odd things that are out there." In this brief but telling comment, sexually transmitted infections are combined with the many unnamed other "things" that are on the street, "out there" (a phrase that establishes distance from a presumably safer environment "in here"). Another woman considered "hepatitis and abuse" to be the most important health concerns for young women and girls on the street. As in the last quote above, this woman's initial discussion of hepatitis gave way to a description of physical violence and then she returned to a broader and more general consideration of sexually transmitted infections, including chlamydia, gonorrhea and genital herpes. It is clear that she considers all these conditions to be equally serious and interwoven rather than distinct. Although hepatitis remained central to this woman's assessment of the health risks of an involvement in prostitution, it is interesting that she admitted to not knowing much about it, saying, "I don't know what the hell it is but it sounds nasty." Hepatitis, then, is a medicalized category for all that is "nasty." It is a way to speak collectively about all that is "out there" waiting to afflict those who are repeatedly exposed to it. In the real lives of sexually exploited youth, HIV/AIDS, other sexually transmitted infections and violence are intertwined and represented in the recollections of exploited youth in collective and connected ways.

These kinds of connections are not often represented in biomedical models of disease or in health education and prevention programs. Instead, individual rates of diseases such as chlamydia (972 per 100,000 young women aged 15–19 years in 1997), gonorrhea (68 per 100,000 young women aged 15–19 years in 1998), and syphilis (0.4 per 100,000 young women aged 15–19 years in 1998) are presented (Statistics Canada 2000), reinforcing the idea that these diseases exist as discrete clinical encounters.[4] As valuable as such discrete measures are for public health planning, this kind of distinction does not correspond to the ways in which sexually exploited girls forge connections among the various health-related challenges. Indeed, biomedical categories of infectious and non-infectious diseases are continuously blurred as the young women with whom we spoke integrated references to drug abuse, depression and unspecified ill-health into their overall discussion of health.

References to drug use were particularly common. One woman introduced drugs into her discussion of health by commenting that when she contracted chlamydia and herpes, she considered it to be the "tax" she had to pay for doing drugs. In response to a general question asking if she had ever been sick, she explained:

> Yeah, with STDs and stuff.... Chlam, umm, something like chlammy? [Chlamydia?] Yeah, that's it, and herpes. I got herpes too. Neither of them will kill me or nothing like that, eh. It's like the tax I got to pay to do the drugs. Just something I got to put up with.

In a very matter-of-fact way, this woman explained that sexually transmitted infections were a necessary, perhaps even inevitable, cost of doing drugs. Others saw it as similarly inevitable but were more direct in discussing drug use as a risk factor rather than on economic cost. For example, one woman whose involvement in prostitution was motivated by her desire for drugs, said,

> I always got the drugs and I always got my fix.... I remember this one time
> sharpening a needle on my finger because it had been so dull.... I'm sure if
> you said to somebody that a needle could possibly have an HIV virus on it, and
> if a junkie has to sit there and decide, they're going to take their chances
> because it's so powerful. When you're ready for a fix and you're going to get it,
> and if I need to sharpen the needle on my thumbnail, I'm going to sharpen
> the needle.

Drug use, like HIV/AIDS, sexually transmitted infections and violence, was rarely discussed on its own. Rather, it was linked with other health-related conditions creating an overarching burden of illness and risk. The same woman quoted above went on to explain that what bothered her most about the health costs of drug use and prostitution was the general "achiness" she felt from the resulting physical discomfort:

> These dirty needles or these damaged needles and dull needles caused
> [swelling]. Like, my arms were a mess and then my feet, we started going in
> my feet. And then wearing high heels on the street and being cold, like, I
> remember just being so bitterly cold and sore from head to toe.

Although the drug abuse was itself a concern, the general achiness was a more poignant memory and perhaps a more pressing health concern at the time.

The only time that drug use was mentioned as an independent health concern without reference to other related conditions was when the women described symptoms of withdrawal, including being "hung over." One woman, for example, claimed that being "hung over" was the most serious of all conditions she experienced during her involvement in prostitution, ranking it higher in severity than the broken ribs and black eye she suffered after one particularly "bad date." It is clear that this drug-induced condition was indeed a severe and painful experience. It impaired her decision-making abilities and ultimately increased her susceptibility to violence, injury and other health-related conditions. Aside from these specific references, drug use was generally integrated conceptually and experientially with other health conditions thus becoming part of an often generalized and overall burden of illness and risk carried by those involved in prostitution. This is significant because the connections among various afflictions disrupt the biomedical categories of disease that define each condition as separately identifiable from the others. Health-related programming that provides integrated resources and treatments in ways that reflect this connectedness are bound to be well received.

"You're on the Streets [and] Just So Tired, You Can't Make Sense of Nothing": Fatigue, Hunger and Hygiene

As significant as the connected references to specific and well-known health conditions are, it is equally significant to consider descriptions of vague ill-health and generalized fatigue that were offered spontaneously and more frequently. One woman, for example, remembers "general pain, hurting all the time" when she recalls her involvement in prostitution. Another woman medicalized not only the personal discomfort and distress she encountered through systems of prostitution but extended this to the entire context of sexual exploitation. Men who constantly want and buy sex from underage girls, she argued, exhibit a "sickness in society." She then went on to explain,

> It's not only like a sickness that I had and all the other girls had. [It was] just this idea that this was OK. It's, that [men] have this idea too. Way down inside it is actually OK to go and buy sex from a thirteen year old. You know what I mean. And you know it's just, some of them are so far gone.

From generalized references to being "sick and tired" and societal "sickness" to more detailed descriptions of the physical achiness that accompanied a lack of sleep, food or safe shelter, the women problematized their exploitation through prostitution by relating it to the general ill-health that very often included both explicit and subtle references to fatigue, sleep deprivation and exhaustion.

In their British Columbia-based study with 201 women and men involved in prostitution in the Capital District, Benoit and Millar (2001: 69) found that 36.6 percent of those surveyed reported having significant sleep disturbances, that almost 13 percent had or were experiencing chronic fatigue-related disorders and that over 12 percent had eating disorders. While it is unclear from our interviews how many women actually had fatigue-related disorders, nineteen (or almost 50 percent) of the forty who discussed health issues in their interviews mentioned fatigue, tiredness and/or sleep deprivation in significant ways. In virtually every case, the women discussing generalized fatigue emphasized the need for safe places to sleep, not only as a way to relieve the routine exhaustion but as a way to take a break from the other pressures of vague ill-health, violence, exploitation and chronic drug use. One woman, for example, rolled all these things together as she discussed the physical difficulties associated with her involvement in prostitution:

> For some people ... like for myself, I never had no pimp or nobody there to, I

was just stingy, you know, on my own. But if I never had those hotel rooms ... or a place to stay, I would have fallen over or collapsed. And I, I did have, actually problems, like, it could have had something to do with exhaustion. 'Cause I'd do drugs for days, like a week at a time, without sleeping. And my kidneys, I've, like screwed up kidneys and they'd fail and I'd end up in hospital. But yeah, exhaustion. I think for people that go real hard that could be a big problem, like, if they don't have a place to stay or whatever.... I'd go for days and, 'cause I'm not eating and I'm just getting high and shitting myself or whatever.

Echoing this call for a safe place to sleep and rest another woman noted,

Yeah, fatigue is a big problem. We sometimes got to work the trick pads, eh? And you can't get no sleep there. Then you're out on the streets [and] just so tired you can't make sense of nothing. Yeah, it's a problem.

Yet another woman stated,

Sometimes I'd be up a day or a half a day and a day, you know what I mean, just 'cause you're constantly getting high or whatever, you don't sleep.... That's, that's something that might help too, just a place to go and sleep and eat a meal. Maybe, just, you know, when you're, when you're rested and when you're fed, maybe it'll just give you an extra kind of, extra minute or two to maybe think about what you're doing. Think about how you actually feel.

For some of the women, this generalized fatigue motivated them to stay in touch with family members who could be counted on to offer safe places for them to catch up on their sleep. As one woman said, "It would all be so much. My body would need to rest. [I'd] need my mind to rest. So I'd go try and stay at my adopted mom's ... for a week or something." For others, the need to rest, eat and replenish their physical fortitude motivated them to seek help from service agencies. One woman spoke positively about her stay at a court-mandated facility because it allowed it her to get as much sleep as she needed to "feel better, feel healthy, like, more like myself again."

Not all such attempts to find safe sleep havens were successful, though. In describing hitting what she called "rock bottom," another woman made a link between her own exhaustion and "service fatigue"[5] that occurred because she thought service providers were becoming frustrated with her recidivism into drugs and prostitution:

I weighed 120 pounds and that for me is, that just does not look good on me. You know ... I had huge bags under my eyes. Nobody even wanted to come near me they were just all fed up with me.

For other women, the search for safe places to sleep and recuperate further exacerbated their exploitation. One woman explained,

> Sometimes I had nowhere to stay.... If I didn't have a pimp, 'cause I stopped dealing with pimps for awhile, if I didn't make any money, I had nowhere to sleep. I had to blow the hotel owner just to have a bed.

She then went on to describe a situation in which a drug dealer became her supplier, not only of narcotics and alcohol but of a place to sleep, and basic necessities such as clothes and food:

> I had one guy specifically ... who owned a club that I could go in. And if I wanted, he had a room downstairs [and] I could sleep there. I could do whatever. He'd give me drugs for free. Feed me booze. He'd buy me clothes.... He was pretty good to me that way. I have to say that, even though all he wanted was sex. But still, you know, when you're in that predicament, you don't have anything or anybody, you're going to reach for whatever you can get.

It is interesting that a reference to sleep is the first thing mentioned as the woman quoted above recounts the resources made available to her through her social street network. The desperation of her circum-stance—her "predicament," as she called it—is made clear in the last two lines of the interview excerpt and it underscores the fact that physical well-being refers not only to the absence of disease but to the availability of life's necessities. A reprieve from fatigue often goes hand-in-hand with the provision of food, shelter, clothes and showers. The same woman quoted above seemed relieved when she found a service for street youth that provided such essentials: "I'd go there and eat and sleep and do my laundry and brush my teeth and certain things I just didn't get to do (while on the street)." And she reported feeling "better" after having been there. Another woman similarly reported that, "I would go to a shelter. I would get my sleep, I would eat and probably stay there for a couple of days. I was using drugs intravenously so I would have to heal my arms."

Given the discomfort resulting from generalized fatigue and inad-equate nutrition that was described so readily by the women, it is clear that there is an ongoing need for services that not only treat specific biomedical conditions but also provide necessary life resources that are essential to restoring a broader sense of well-being. We can conclude that an intersectoral approach that provides very specific medical treat-ment and information as well as more generalized assistance has a great deal to offer. Such an approach (which was endorsed by several of the service providers interviewed) would redress not only the physical but also the emotional costs of the exploitation of prostitution.

"The General Wear and Tear of the Spirit": Emotional Health and Social Balance

"I'm a nut," said one woman as she began her interview and explained the effects that her involvement in prostitution had on her. "I had, like, a breakdown," said another as she recalled the point at which she decided to leave the streets. "I kind of fell apart," said one more, while still another reflected on her desire to commit suicide as a way to escape the streets. These statements are characteristic of many others that reflect the challenges that ongoing sexual exploitation presented to the emotional health of women with whom we spoke. Indeed, references to emotional health—described by one woman as "a kind of balance"—figured more prominently in the interviews than references to physical health. It was not that the women discounted their physical health, but they recognized connections between the two so that the physical was frequently subsumed within broader and more psychologically focused discussions of what it meant to "just be alright," as one woman put it.[6] Emotional balance and health were, for the most part, cast in terms of the women's psychological stability, physical well-being and personal agency. Emotional distress was seen to result, as one woman claimed, from "the general wear and tear of ... the spirit" and this, in turn, presented great challenges to their physical and psychological well-being.

Although very few women interviewed used the word "depression," many described having extremely low self-esteem and this obviously exacted a physical and emotional toll. Indeed, a low, and in some cases even missing, self-regard underlies many of the stories of emotional distress and physical ill-health. One woman recalled grieving the death of a family member while being exploited through prostitution, and the emotional costs were clear: "I didn't care what was going on. I could go all week without showering and it wouldn't bother me. I had no self-esteem. I didn't eat properly [and] I did drugs." Another woman recalled the devastating effect that a childhood rape had on her sense of self-worth, saying,

> For years after that, I thought it was me ... and my slutiness that made the gang rape happen. And I never saw myself as the victim in this scenario. It was completely my fault. I was a horrible person. I was just, like, I was a slut and a whore.

Several women attributed subsequent illnesses, "breakdowns" and violent injuries to their personal neglect and low self-esteem. They said that they had lost control over their lives and as a result they felt meaningless to others and to themselves.

Having a discernible influence over one's life, even though such influences are always circumscribed, is perhaps one of the key and central aspects to maintaining emotional health for the socially marginalized, including sexually exploited youth. In their studies of social and personal agency, researchers and practitioners from many fields have long debated how such a sense of influence or control should be defined and understood. There are those who eschew specificity and define agency broadly as the ability to affect the course of one's own life (e.g., Hekman 1995) while others are more concerned with the particular degree of economic independence one exercises (e.g., Hartmann 1981). Still others focus more theoretically on how agency can be accommodated within the seemingly constraining structures of society (e.g., McNay 2000; Sztompka 1994). Consistently underlying these theories, though, is the idea that agency involves a will to act and an ability to address, even in small and apparently mundane ways, prevailing life conditions. This common idea is the factor of greatest relevance to a discussion of health and well-being. As many of the women repeatedly indicated, taking steps to affect or direct aspects of their lives, regardless of how small or ostensibly insignificant those aspects might be, resulted in greater feelings of self-worth and ultimately led to a greater sense of balance, integrity and general health.

"I've always been a fighter. I've always stood up for myself," said one woman as she expressed a sense of self-determination that also resonated in the statement of another woman who noted, "I've always had this thing where, you know, I needed to be self-sufficient. I'm taking care of myself, nobody takes care of me, I take care of myself." These women clearly pride themselves on their ability to act willingly on their own behalf and to stand up for themselves, because they believe they are worthy of such actions. Other women were less direct in referring to their own agency but acknowledged that their ability to read their "instincts" or "feelings" kept them safe and healthy. For one woman, this ability was a matter of life and death: "You got to have them feelings if you're on the street. If you don't got them, you die." Clearly, having the willingness, opportunity and capability to respond, even in small ways, to the surrounding social conditions allows exploited youth to feel psychologically and physically secure.

The women repeatedly argued that when the violence of the streets, the exploitation of youth prostitution or the coercion of some (usually court-mandated) programs intercede and reduce the influence that they can exert over the course of their own lives, a form of distress often results. And this distress frequently takes a medicalized form. As one woman so succinctly stated, "[The younger girls get] beat if they don't get the boyfriends their money or whatever and, you know, getting mentally fucked up because they have no control over their life." One woman—who reported feeling extremely constricted by the fatigue she experienced from her involvement in prostitution and by the ongoing threat of violence and assault—said that the only way she could gain a sense of control was to physically hurt herself:

> If I see that my body's marked up, the pain is gone. If I see blood, the pain's gone. But if, if I bottle up so much hurt, like, I go … ballistic. There are times I, I tried smashing my head against the window, tried to break the window with my forehead.… Recently, in September, I just slit my wrist. I blacked out on drinking.… I was, like, on coke and drinking and stuff … and then there was blood everywhere. And then the ambulance had to come and get me and they, they threw me on the cop car because I didn't want to go with the ambulance. I had to get six stitches.

This litany of injuries resulted from the pent-up frustration brought on by the limited influence this woman felt she had over her own life circumstances. Of course, drug use exacerbated her sense of lost control as it did in so many other women's lives. In fact, some women noted that because drug use impaired their abilities to purposefully maintain their safety and health, they did not use drugs while they were working. Negative emotions, such as anger, also frequently compromised the women's sense of agency and ultimately their well-being. It therefore became clear that when an individual's sense of personal agency is challenged by ongoing abuse, violation, exploitation, fatigue, anger or a myriad of other factors so commonly experienced by youth involved in prostitution, psychological well-being can suffer. This, in turn, exacerbates physical illnesses and injuries.

"Running Your Own Life": Program Implications

The program implications of these findings concerning emotional health and personal agency are important. Those programs that offered the women the opportunity to increase the influence over their own life were more positively received than were those that were more rigid. One woman explained,

> You know, I think, I hate to say it, but I think the [program] that actually helped me was AA and NA. The ones that ... you went in there on your own choice. And you had other people around you that were there from their own choices, just kinda shared their experiences in a loving way. And I'm not saying that, like there's a lot of sick people in AA and NA and I learned that too. There was a lot of creepy old guys asking me there, too.... It's everywhere but, um, but that kind of atmosphere of kind of self-healing, like, you know what I mean, like doing it at your own pace kind of, I don't know, it just gives you a lot more honour and respect of, you know, running your own life kind-of-thing. And definitely like now, like after I was off the street, places like this [agency] have done major things for me. Like that's probably why I'm still off ... 'cause this place really has given me a voice. Has given me power. Like I've got things to do here, you know. I've got purpose here. There's other people that need to have like almost like a role model, and be shown, like, you can get off the street you know and life can be good and you know, the anger does go away.

The importance of self-healing and influencing the pace and direction of the program (interpreted by the woman quoted above as a kind of power) also informed one woman's account of what she did not like about one particular addictions program, namely its rigidity and perceived abusiveness:

> I don't believe in their philosophy. Their philosophy is they're going to beat you down.... [Tough love] is what they call it but that's bullshit. Tough love is not sitting me up ... and making me describe in detail about how I fucked a forty-year-old man for, like, thirty bucks.... They forced me into [talking about it].... In graphic detail right down to the smell. So needless to say, I don't like [that program]. I found it mentally abusive, personally.

This same woman similarly expressed concerns about the lack of influence she had over her own schedule in one court-mandated facility for addiction, saying,

> It's, like, "You're going to bed now! You're going to wake up now! You're going to eat now!" You know, for somebody whose been up all night and sleeping all day, and eating every once in awhile, having three meals and two snacks shoved down your throat ... usually doesn't go over very well. So ... they don't give you time to flip your schedule around, they just flip it for you.

She then contrasted this to another secure care facility that allowed more mobility, granted more opportunity for the girls to direct their own actions:

> When [the second secure facility]opened up, it was perfect. It really was.... If we wanted to go [to] the washroom, we didn't have to ask anybody, we just

went. Like, I mean, it was locked up.... We couldn't leave the building, but as far as I wanted to go to my room, all I had to do, if I was going to be there for more than two minutes, is just let a staff know.

Having some influence, even if it is saying when they will go to the washroom, is a desirable component of programming. As we continue to try to assist exploited youth to deal with the challenges in their lives, including the health-related challenges, we would be well advised to remember that a sense of personal control, purpose and influence can have tremendously positive effects.

"I Went to See the Nurse and They Popped Me Full of Pills ... But They Never Told Me or Talked to Me About It": Health-Seeking Activities

Although none of the women mentioned a medically oriented service when asked what resources helped them during their involvement in prostitution, many showed little hesitation to seek medical assistance when necessary. One woman spoke fondly of her family physician who assisted her in contacting other organizations. Several Saskatchewan participants reported being quite satisfied with a particular clinic; as one woman said, "I mean, you know, it's a clinic not an amusement park, eh. But, you know, it's OK. Nobody's ever been shitty to me there or nothing like that." Even recollections of detox centres were often positive:

> All these social workers weren't doing me a whole lot of good, so mom got me in to see this psychiatrist.... My mom thought I had bipolar disorder or something like that. And after an hour with the psychiatrist, he said to my mom, "she doesn't have bipolar disorder ... she's a drug addict and she's an alcoholic." So they whisked me off ... to a detox centre. [It was] one of the many times of being in detox. I spent a lot of time after that in detox. It was kind of a refuge. [That] is what it became for me.... The detox I went to was in my home town and my roommate became my best friend.... She was a hooker and junkie from [another city] and we became best friends. And she cared about me, and she thought, you know, her and I are going to get cleaned up together.

In contrast, other women, though still showing no hesitancy to seek medical assistance, reported less positive experiences with medical care. One woman spoke very harshly about the psychological counselling offered through some exit programs, doubting counsellors' claims of confidentiality. Another woman spoke equally harshly about the stagnation that she believes sets in through addictions programs such as Alcoholics Anonymous and Narcotics Anonymous:

> Well, sitting around day after day, listening to all these people talking, telling their [stories].... There's some people that get obsessed with AA and NA. And they make it their life. And everyday [they] got to go to a meeting.... And I remember thinking, I don't want to be like that. I don't want to be dependent on going to some stupid AA meeting or NA meeting. I just can't do that. And I got really fed up with listening to these people with these same problems and it seemed like they just ... never moved forward. They just ... got to AA, you got sober and then you just sat around a table and drank coffee and bitched for the rest of your life. And I thought, na.

One more woman was quite perturbed when she sought treatment for a sexually transmitted infection while in a secure care facility. Although she received medication, she was never given any information about the infection, the medication or the course of treatment she was to follow:

> I think [I had] STDs twice but you know what, I have no idea what it was. I went into [secure care], I went to see the, ah, nurse and they popped me full of pills and I don't even have no idea why and I'm thinking back now, I'm thinking that's probably why but I have no idea. They never, they never actually even told me or talked to me about it. Strange, eh?

The dissatisfaction with medical care described by these women, and the eight others like them who expressed similar concerns, is based in part on the fact that they were not given the opportunity to influence the course of their treatment or recovery. As noted in the previous section, denying marginalized and exploited youth the opportunity to contribute to the maintenance or restoration of their physical and emotional health can be more detrimental than helpful. It is perhaps this fear of losing the little control that they do have over their lives that keeps many of the young women from seeking medical attention when they are pregnant. Indeed, one of the only times that the women with whom we spoke expressed anxiety and trepidation about seeking medical assistance was when they were pregnant. The fear of having their children taken from them—and losing the opportunity to meaningfully contribute to their children's lives—was significant, as was the prevailing anxiety about abortion. Therefore, health care programming, like more general programming aimed at assisting youth involved in prostitution, should include the youth as active participants in their own recovery; this approach will undoubtedly be better received than one that is more regulated, pre-determined and impersonal.

Conclusion

The focus of this chapter has been on the health-related information that emerged through our discussions with forty-seven young women who have first-hand knowledge of the challenges faced by sexually exploited youth through systems of prostitution. It is clear from our interviews that while the traditional focus on sexual health—including HIV/AIDS and sexually transmitted infections—is important, it is equally important to consider other health-related challenges facing young women who are involved in prostitution. Often, specific medical conditions, such as physical injuries and sexually transmitted infections, are couched in broader understandings and experiences of fatigue, low self-esteem and a general feeling of being "down." Therefore, health-related programming that is combined with the provision of shelter, food and clothing would be well situated to address the more far reaching challenges to the young women's sustained well-being. Those programs that offer the young women an opportunity to influence the course of their recovery would not only help to relieve specific medical conditions but it would also attend to the connections that the young women forge among those conditions. Ultimately, such an approach might even redress underlying feelings of worthlessness that so often perpetuate damaging cycles of exploitation and ill-health.

Notes

1. By "systems of prostitution" I mean the various degrees of institutionalization that characterize the sale of sex for money or consideration. This term encompasses the following: transnational and highly organized sex trafficking; locally known and well-established prostitute and pimp networks that are located in escort agencies, massage parlours, on the streets, and other sites; as well as more spontaneous and less predictable forms of prostitution. These various "systems" often operate according to different rules and patterns but there are commonalities. The exploitation of children and youth occurs within all these systems.

2. As stated earlier, because each provincial research team had its own focus, explicit and pre-determined questions about health status and health-seeking behaviours were asked only in Saskatchewan; however, it is significant to note that references to health-related issues arose in forty of the forty-seven interviews with experiential youth and in twenty-two of the interviews with service providers.

3. Street youth is defined by Miller et al. (2002) as those youth, under the age of twenty-four years, who spend at least ten hours per day on the street, and/or at least two nights per week on the street, and who identify their primary

social network as being other street-involved youth and adults. It includes those youth exploited through prostitution but is not limited to them.

4. It is important to note that young women in Canada, and elsewhere, are more likely to contract a sexually transmitted disease than are young men in the same age category. In 1997, for example, "the number of reported cases of chlamydia was seven times higher for women aged 15–19 than for men in the same age group. Similarly, there were nearly three times as many gonorrhea cases and four times as many syphilis cases among women as among men in this age range" (Statistics Canada 2000: 51). Although these statistics are, in part, explained by the fact that girls utilize health care facilities more than boys and therefore have more opportunities to be tested, this variance is nonetheless worth considering seriously.

5. "Service fatigue" is occasionally discussed in select social work literature (e.g., Fisher and Harrison 1997; Inciardi, Lockwood and Pottieger 1993) and refers to the fatigue or "burnout" of service providers who deal with sexually exploited youth.

6. There have been some excellent critiques of the division between physical and emotional health (e.g., Adelson 2000; Lock and Scheper-Hughes 1990; Lyon and Barbalet 1994; Morris 1998), and for the most part the views of the women participating in this study support those critiques.

Chapter Five

The Protective Confinement of Girls Involved in Prostitution
Potential Problems in Current Regimes[1]

Karen Busby

A Curious and Contradictory Place in Law

Until recently prostitution-related laws have focused almost exclusively on controlling and regulating girls and women. Criminal laws like vagrancy laws, regulatory laws like contagious disease control regimes, and international conventions like the *International Convention for the Suppression of the Traffic in Women and Children*, either expressly or in practice only applied to females (Diduck and Wilson 1997). Early juvenile justice policies in Canada and the United States criminalized female sexual behaviour, and girls were prosecuted "almost exclusively for moral offences, that is, real or suspected sexual behavior" (Abrams and Curran 2000: 49; Brock 1998; Backhouse 1984). In contrast, men and boys involved in prostitution and johns and pimps were ignored in law or not subject to prosecution (Lefler 1999).

Although most Canadian prostitution-related laws are now gender-neutral and some jurisdictions have adopted practices designed to charge johns, not prostitutes, most prostitution-related charges are against women. Charging pimps and johns remains extremely difficult because of the reluctance of those they exploit to testify against them, or their lack of credibility within the criminal justice system if they do agree to testify (Federal/Provincial/Territorial Working Group on Prostitution 1998). Additionally the practice of using female police officers, who of course will be adults, working undercover as prostitutes will not capture johns who seek minors. A gender bias also exists with respect to sentencing disparities: 39 percent of women but only 3 percent of men convicted under the communicating for prostitution provisions in the *Criminal Code* received jail sentences, and women are significantly more likely to be detained in custody after arrest than men (Duchesne 1997).

Girls involved in prostitution have always occupied a curious and contradictory place in criminal law because they are treated as both perpetrators and victims (Sullivan 1986; Strange and Loo 1997). Lowman (1987: 111) describes this as a "contradiction recurrent over the past 200 years where punishment and treatment are confused." Currently, children involved in prostitution can be charged with prostitution-related offences under the federal criminal laws, like communicating for the purposes of prostitution, and for activities that are associated with street life, like drug possession. These charges are frequently laid because police officers working undercover can gather the evidence. On the other hand, the pimps and johns who exploit girls can be charged with prostitution-related *Criminal Code* offences, including offences specifically aimed at protecting minors, like procuring for prostitution or engaging in prostitution with someone under eighteen. However, gathering evidence for these cases is very difficult and therefore charges against those who exploit minors are almost never laid. The contradiction can also be found in sentencing practices. Sentences for young offenders convicted of communication offences tended to be harsher than for adults similarly charged (Van Brunschot 1995).

The recommendations of the Badgley Report (1984), a federally funded report of a special committee charged with undertaking research and consultations across Canada on the sexual abuse of children, managed to combine the offender and victim approaches. It stated that "there were no effective means of stopping the demonstrated harms that … children and youths [involved in prostitution] bring upon themselves. For these reasons, the Committee believed that the implementation of criminal sanctions against these youths and children *must be made a legal possibility by creating an offence so that social intervention can take place*" [emphasis added] (Badgley 1984: 1046). While this widely-criticized recommendation (Department of Justice 1989; Fraser 1985; Brannigan and Fleischman 1989; Lowman 1987) was not implemented, the Badgley Report is a stark reminder that slippage between criminal justice and social welfare responses—where punishment is seen as help—continues to be advocated.

Currently, in Canada various intervention strategies can be used to protect children exploited through prostitution: these include general provincial child protection legislation (often called the *Child and Family Services Act* or the *Child Welfare Act* [CFSAs]), and specific legislative initiatives, such as Alberta's *Protection of Children Involved in Prostitution Act* (PCHIP) and British Columbia's *Secure Care Act* (SCA), which is not yet in force. PCHIP-like legislation has also been introduced in Saskatchewan, Nova Scotia and Ontario although none of these bills have passed into law. (See the Appendix to this chapter on provincial child protection statutes.) Legislated intervention strategies include involuntary apprehension and detention of minors involved in prostitution, provincial charges against pimps and johns, novel sentencing provisions like vehicle seizures, protective orders to minimize contact between minors and those who facilitate their exploitation and funding for voluntary programs for street-involved youth.

This chapter focuses on the controversial strategy of protective confinement or secure care (that is, involuntary or coercive holding) for girls involved in prostitution under child protection legislation. I will outline the main features of these regimes, review the emergency apprehension and confinement provisions in traditional CFSAs and contrast these provisions with the recently enacted PCHIP and SCA regimes. This review will also outline some problems, including whether the proper test is being used to justify emergency apprehensions and whether potential *Canadian Charter of Rights and Freedoms* (*Charter*) violations arise. It will conclude with an analysis of the efficacy of these regimes with a particular focus on whether the potential *Charter* rights violations can be justified as a reasonable limit in a free and democratic society.

As girls are far more likely than boys to be apprehended and detained under child protection regimes for prostitution-related activities, female nouns and pronouns will be used sometimes in this chapter. This different treatment of girls and boys may occur because boys become involved in prostitution at an older age than girls, fewer boys than girls are involved, and boys are less likely to work on the street and therefore do not attract as much police and social work attention. Different treatment may also simply be a current-day manifestation of the historical phenomena of regulating girls' sexual behavior.

Overview of Apprehension and Detention Regimes

The traditional CFSA models vary in their fine details from province to province, but almost all permit the police and child protection workers to apprehend and detain a "child in need of protection," which the statutes define as a child whose "life, health or emotional well-being is endangered." CFSAs list specific examples of circumstances where a child would be in need of protection. These examples always include children who are being sexually abused and many explicitly refer to children who are sexually exploited or involved in prostitution or who use alcohol or non-therapeutic drugs. In some provinces, children are covered by child protection legislation until they turn sixteen, and in others until they turn eighteen. A child in need of protection can be apprehended either with or without court order. Warrantless searches are permitted for a child who may be in "immediate danger." Most CFSAs provide that a child who is already in care may be apprehended, if that child leaves without permission, and may be returned to the agency or foster home. However CFSAs usually provide that a child in need of protection cannot be held at a detention centre designed for young offenders, although some provide that secure care facilities which restrict liberty can be used where children have mental disorders and threaten to harm themselves or others.[2] Sixty-three percent of the women interviewed for this project were already in care when they became involved in prostitution. All but four of the Manitoba women interviewed had been apprehended under child protection legislation on an emergency basis for very serious problems, like a life-threatening drug overdose, after becoming involved in prostitution. Agencies are required to make an application to a court within four days of the apprehension to determine whether the child is in need of protection. Agencies can apply for orders to prevent contact between apprehended children and those who have or may have abused them; it is a provincial offence for anyone to, for example, help a child leave the premises where a child has been placed.

Although both Alberta and British Columbia have traditional CFSAs and therefore already have apprehension, detention and other powers which can be used to protect girls exploited in prostitution, these provinces have also adopted more specific legislation. PCHIP is solely concerned with children engaging or attempting to engage in prostitution whereas the SCA covers children who present a "high risk of serious harm or injury" resulting from severe substance misuse or sexual exploitation.

PCHIP permits police and social workers to apprehend anyone under eighteen who is involved in prostitution either after obtaining a court order or, in emergency situations, without such an order. It appears that most PCHIP apprehensions occur without a prior court order. Warrantless searches of places where these children may be found are permitted. The children may be held for five days if the child welfare authorities consider this necessary to ensure their safety and to assess the child, including tests for drug and alcohol use, sexually transmitted diseases, HIV and pregnancy. Section 2(12) of PCHIP provides that child welfare authorities "must" appear in court to "show cause," which means they must provide evidence to the court as to why the confinement under the emergency provisions was necessary. However section 2.1(2) (which was added in 2000) modifies the mandatory nature of this provision by stating that "if a show cause hearing has not been held ... a child ... may ask ... the Court to review" the confinement. In practice, it appears that show cause hearings are not frequently held (Border 2000; Koshan 2001). Child welfare authorities must advise children apprehended under PCHIP that they can be represented by counsel at these hearings and must provide them with the phone number for a legal aid office. However, show cause hearings are not statutorily required for either court-ordered apprehensions or warrantless searches. After the initial five-day period, child welfare authorities can ask a judge to order that a child be confined for twenty-one days and, on the expiry of this period, can extend the confinement for an additional twenty-one days. Most children are released after the initial period of apprehension although many children have been apprehended repeatedly, including one girl who was apprehended at least seventeen times (Border 2000; Koshan 2001).[3] No contact orders can be obtained, and anyone who involves children in prostitution can be charged with an offence under the act. The SCA provisions are similar to PCHIP.

In the majority of cases, children apprehended under CFSAs are at risk of being harmed by their parents or other family members and do not have strong opinions about the apprehensions. In contrast, PCHIP apprehensions occur to protect girls from actions in which they engage themselves. (Although non-familial third parties are involved in their exploitation, these third parties are difficult to identify and, unlike parents, would not have the right to contest the apprehension.) The girls are usually opposed to the apprehensions. Few children being apprehended from their parents will take action to avoid apprehension, whereas girls who fear being apprehended under protective confinement legislation may be reluctant to access voluntary services and can be expected to take evasive action to avoid detection. Some of the key differences, then, between the CFSA regime and the PCHIP and SCA regimes are that the latter is better designed to ensure that those who are apprehended can be held against their will, whereas that is not a particular concern under CFSAs. As well, apprehensions under the CFSA regime will always be subject to judicial oversight, whereas PCHIP apprehensions are often not reviewed. While it is not mandated by the legislation, girls apprehended under PCHIP may be held in facilities that are used to house only them and therefore may receive specialized services during and after the period of detention. The passage of PCHIP may also indicate a political will to address the exploitation of girls in prostitution: while it is not mandated by legislation, since it became law more money has been allocated for non-governmental helping programs. Other differences between the two regimes will be described later.

It appears that PCHIP legislation treads a fine line between youth protection and undue abrogation of people's rights. The constitutionality of PCHIP was challenged on a number of grounds in the *Alberta* v. *K.B.* case. Portions of the act were struck down by the Provincial Court judge who first heard the case but this decision was overturned by a Court of Queen's Bench judge who held that PCHIP was constitutional. While the courts' decisions on the constitutional and other issues considered in the *KB* case are examined here, it is important to recognize that, unlike Supreme Court of Canada decisions, these lower court decisions do not have significant precedential effects and another Queen's Bench judge is free to come to a different conclusion on the constitutionality of the legislation. PCHIP has not been subject to a challenge before the Alberta Court of Appeal or the Supreme Court of Canada. Additionally, as the courts in the *K.B.* case had almost no evidence before them on how PCHIP actually operated, the court's decision might be different if this evidence were presented.

The Test For Emergency Apprehension

The CFSA Test of "Serious Risk of Harm"
When is it appropriate to apprehend children without pre-authorization? With the passage of PCHIP and SCA, this question has become an even more important one than in the past.

CFSAs, PCHIP and SCA all permit a judge to pre-authorize the apprehension of children. About 50 percent of the apprehensions under CFSAs are pre-approved by a judge, whereas almost all of the girls apprehended and detained under PCHIP are apprehended on an emergency basis without pre-authorization and most are released after the initial period of confinement (Border 2000; Koshan 2001). For this reason, I will focus on emergency apprehensions.

Emergency apprehensions are permitted under traditional CFSAs where there are "reasonable and probable grounds [to believe that] ... a child is in need of protection." The "child is in need of protection" threshold for emergency apprehensions under the Manitoba CFSA was challenged in the *K.L.W.* v. *Winnipeg Child and Family Services* case. (As the *K.L.W.* case was decided by the Supreme Court of Canada, it is a precedent that must be applied across Canada when similar laws are being considered or interpreted.) In that case, a baby was apprehended at the hospital by child protection authorities a few hours after birth. The mother's other children were already in care. The agency considered that immediate apprehension of the newborn was necessary as the mother had not addressed the problems (addictions and continuing contact with an abusive partner) which had created the need for these apprehensions. The mother's constitutional challenge asserted that the statute authorizing the apprehension set too low a threshold for apprehensions which had not been pre-authorized by a judge and therefore violated parents' rights to liberty and security as protected by the *Charter*. In particular, the mother argued that the danger had to be imminent (which it could not be if the parent and child were both in the hospital) before an apprehension that had not been pre-authorized was permissible.

As a result of this challenge, the Supreme Court of Canada held that parents' *Charter* rights had to be balanced against children's rights and that the decision-making processes used by the child protection workers had to be examined to determine if they were fundamentally just in all the circumstances. The Court upheld the constitutionality of apprehensions which are not pre-authorized, even in non-emergency situations, where there is a "serious risk of harm." More specifically, the Court stated that, as legislatures could mandate *preventative* as well as *protective* state intervention regarding children, a statute which did not require proof of "imminent harm" would still survive a constitutional challenge. (Two of the seven judges who heard this case dissented from this conclusion and held that apprehensions which were not preauthorized were constitutionally valid only in emergency situations. In their view, this form of apprehension had to be a "measure of last resort.") However the Court also set out three protections for parents regarding apprehensions that were not pre-authorized by a judge: 1) apprehensions should be used only as a last resort where no less disruptive means were available; 2) judicial review of the apprehension had to be prompt and fair; 3) courts can impose sanctions to deter the authorities from failing to meet legislative standards. Thus, some safeguards were built into the process.

The PCHIP and SCA Tests: Are They Different From the CFSA Test?

Following the *K.L.W.* case, it is clear that legislation that permits children to be apprehended to prevent harm or protect against harm without prior judicial authorization will not violate the *Charter* provided, amongst other things, the legislative standard for apprehension is met. What is the legislative standard or threshold for emergency apprehension under PCHIP and SCA? More particularly, can girls be apprehended if a police officer or social worker believes that they are involved in prostitution, or is evidence of something more than simple involvement required? Another way of approaching this issue is to consider whether PCHIP and SCA apprehensions are just protective or are they, like general child protection legislation, intended to protect children from immediate (protective) and future (preventative) harm.

The Queen's Bench decision in the *K.B.* case held (at para.72) that a child could be apprehended on an emergency basis if there are grounds to believe that she was "engag[ed] in an inherently dangerous activity such as prostitution." In other words, belief that she is involved in prostitution is all that is required. However, strong arguments can be made that something more than simple involvement in prostitution is required. The precise statutory language used in PCHIP only permits emergency apprehensions and involuntary confinements when "the child's life and safety is seriously and imminently endangered because the child has been engaged in prostitution." Similarly the SCA permits apprehensions and detention of minors without prior authorization only if three conditions are established: there is an "immediate risk of serious harm"; less intrusive measures are not available; and "detainment is necessary to ensure the child's safety."

If simple involvement in prostitution was sufficient to ground a PCHIP apprehension, the words "seriously and imminently endangered" are without meaning. The phrase "seriously ... endangered" suggests more than a "serious risk of harm." Unlike the legislation considered in the *K.L.W.* case, where apprehension took place under a CFSA, imminency *is* a specific legislative requirement in PCHIP. Thus, the "seriously and imminently endangered" requirement could indicate a higher threshold[4] for apprehension and detention of minors under PCHIP than the "serious risk of harm" test established by the Supreme Court of Canada for CFSA apprehensions. Similarly, the SCA provisions incorporate immediacy and necessity requirements. In the *K.L.W.* case, the Supreme Court of Canada held that adherence to the legislative standard for apprehensions and detentions that are not pre-authorized by a judge is an important safeguard against the abuse of power. Therefore, apprehending agents and lower court judges should pay close attention to the precise requirements of the statute.

Rationales for a Higher Threshold

Many reports[5] of government committees, non-governmental organizations and researchers note that girls involved in prostitution approach voluntary services with caution because they are suspicious of authority figures and they will take evasive action to avoid apprehension. These reports either reject involuntary confinement outright or do not even consider whether it should be used. Some reports note how involuntary apprehensions have been misused. For example, the Alberta Children's Advocate[6] reported in 1993 that the use of secure treatment for children with behavioural disorders (which was permitted under child protection legislation) was often used as a "social control mechanism for hard-to-handle youth." He found that secure treatment was being used, contrary to the statute, to deal with lifestyle issues such as running away and street gang association when other options were not available.

Some special committees commissioned by legislators to advise on issues related to children involved in prostitution recommended involuntary confinement. All of these reports noted how involuntary regimes can alienate those whom they are intended to assist and stated that they should be used only as a last resort, as a protective measure. The Alberta Task Force on Children Involved in Prostitution, established by the Minister of Family and Social Services, noted that "outreach activities to establish a rapport with children ... and develop a trusting relationship are the key" (1997: 8). It recommended a continuum of services including temporary accommodations and outreach services. Locked confinement was recommended, as part of this continuum, only where the youth "are a danger to themselves or others." Use of the "seriously and imminently endangered" threshold for emergency apprehensions under PCHIP helps ensure that the apprehension provisions are not misused, as the secure treatment provisions had been, and reflects the Task Force's end-of-the-continuum recommendation.

The *Secure Care Working Group Report* (British Columbia Ministry for Children and Families 1998) in British Columbia (appointed by the Minister of Children and Families) also acknowledged that secure care can be misused: it states that secure care should be used for children "who are at extremely high risk of harm" and in "imminent" and "extreme danger," and that it had to be implemented with "*extreme caution*" (emphasis in original). In contrast, the report of the [British Columbia] Assistant Deputy Ministers' Committee on Prostitution and the Sexual Exploitation of Youth (2000), which repeatedly acknowledged the reluctance of youth to access services because of the fear of reprisals and emphasized a comprehensive multi-service agency approach, maintained a deafening silence on whether secure care should be used and did not even list the Secure Care Working Group Report in its extensive list of references. Given the Working Group's cautious support, and the Assistant Deputy Minister's implicit lack of support, for secure care, it is not surprising that the necessity and immediacy requirements are repeated throughout the SCA for all apprehension and continuing involuntary confinement decisions.

The Federal/Provincial/Territorial Working Group on Prostitution (1998: 28) (established by deputy ministers responsible for justice) stated that secure treatment "would probably alienate" the child and that even where detention might be necessary to prevent "serious bodily harm to himself/herself or another person" it "should only occur in an extremely selective manner."

The Special Committee to Prevent the Abuse and Exploitation of Children Through the Sex Trade (appointed by the Saskatchewan Legislative Assembly) heard significant opposition to a secure care regime during its community consultations, in part because "the picture of residential schools comes back" (2001: 25). Thus, while that committee favoured implementation of a secure-care regime on a trial basis, it too recommended that apprehensions should be limited to situations of *"imminent danger* (i.e., life and death circumstances)" [emphasis in the original] (27). The draft bill recommended by this committee permits emergency apprehensions only where the child is "seriously and imminently endangered." (Similar language was used in the PCHIP-like private members bills introduced in Nova Scotia, Saskatchewan and Ontario but not in the government-sponsored legislation introduced in Ontario.)

Thus, all of the legislative and ministerial reports that recommended use of protective confinement saw it not as a preventative form of early intervention but as a protective and last resort measure. It seems, therefore, that PCHIP's "seriously and imminently endangered" threshold for emergency apprehensions and SCA's necessity and immediacy requirements for all apprehensions were purposely chosen by legislators to ensure that involuntary apprehensions were only used in extraordinary situations or under judicial supervision. Watering down the legislative language, and thereby the standards, by those who implement the legislation renders ineffective an important limitation set by the legislature on the use of emergency involuntary confinement.

Potential Misuses of a Lower Threshold

There is some evidence that the police in Alberta have apprehended and detained girls when there is no heightened and immediate risk like excessive drug use or threats from a pimp. According to their lawyer, Bina Border (Border 2000), one of the apprehended seventeen-year-old respondents in the *K.B.* case had been on the street earlier on the day she was apprehended. An officer had approached her and suggested that she go home. About an hour later the officer showed up at the apartment she shared with another girl. One girl was sleeping; the other was watching television. Neither of them was under the influence of drugs or alcohol or attempting to engage in prostitution. One girl denied that she had ever been involved in prostitution. The officer did not have a warrant but told the girl who answered the door that if he was not let in voluntarily, he would invoke PCHIP warrantless entry powers. During the search, the officer dumped out the contents of the girls' purses, which included condoms and a marijuana pipe. Both girls were apprehended. The only account reported in the Queen's Bench judgment (para. 71) is the evidence of the Director of Child Welfare who testified that the police went to an apartment "to look for stolen property, found the two children in a dirty apartment, with a mattress on the floor and condoms and drug paraphernalia strewn about." The Queen's Bench judge stated (para. 71) that these facts "illustrate why authorities should have the ability to apprehend a child engaging in prostitution in emergency situations." The show cause hearing, which was adjourned pending the constitutional challenge, was not resumed in the *K.B.* case.

Apprehension in the circumstances described by Border suggests that the threshold of "serious and imminent danger because the child is engaging in prostitution" is not always used by the police or social workers. If girls are being apprehended even though they do not face imminent and serious endangerment, the police may be failing to meet the legislative standards for apprehension and could be called to account for this failure. If the threshold for apprehension is lowered through police and social work practices, bureaucratic regulation and judicial interpretation, and if show cause hearings are not held to monitor these practices, PCHIP and SCA risk becoming another social-control mechanism for hard-to-handle children and not the extraordinary protective measure they were intended to be.

Potential *Charter* Violations

It is quite possible that the PCHIP violates *Charter* freedoms and rights, although this has not yet been clearly demonstrated. I will look at this issue as it affects three areas: apprehension and searches, places of detention and medical treatment.

The Canadian *Charter of Rights and Freedoms* provides that everyone has certain fundamental rights and freedoms like freedom of religion (section 2); the right to life, liberty and the security of the person (section 7); the right to be secure against unreasonable search or seizure (section 8); freedom from arbitrary detention (section 9); the right to be informed of the right to retain and instruct counsel upon detention (section 10); and the right to be treated equal before the law without discrimination (section 15). Some of these rights have internal limitations. For example, the right to life, liberty and security of the person can be taken away from a person if the deprivation is "in accordance with the principles of fundamental justice." This provision requires that the procedures used to decide whether the deprivation is warranted must be fair and the deprivation itself must not be disproportionate to the act that led to the deprivation. Searches are permitted as long as they are not "unreasonable"; detentions are permitted as long as they are not "arbitrary." Section 1 creates a general limit on all *Charter* rights and freedoms stating that they can be subject to "reasonable limits … as can be demonstrably justified in a free and democratic society."

Some PCHIP and SCA provisions may violate *Charter* rights. Given space limitations, the extensive jurisprudence on the nature of the *Charter* rights under discussion, including internal limitations, are not discussed in any detail. As well, the section 1 analysis is preliminary only, outlining one novel argument concerning the proportionality of the legislation.

Reviewing Apprehensions and Searches

Most CFSAs and both PCHIP and SCA require the agency to make an application to a judge or independent tribunal within a short period (usually less than a week) to justify or show cause for the emergency apprehension and, if it is being sought, continued detention. No show cause hearings are required under PCHIP if the initial apprehension and detention is permitted by court order (even though the child was not present at this hearing) or if the child is not confined after detention. CFSAs, PCHIP and SCA permit the police or social workers to search premises without first obtaining a search warrant if there is reason to believe that a child on the premises is in serious and imminent danger. None of the statutes provide for a post-warrant judicial review of the necessity of the search, either as a mandatory justification or "show cause" requirement, or on the application of an affected person. Does the failure of PCHIP to provide affected children and others with a review mechanism for pre-authorized apprehensions and warrantless searches give rise to constitutional violations?

Section 8 of the *Charter* gives everyone the right to be secure from "unreasonable searches and seizures." The Supreme Court of Canada held in the *Feeney* case that "a warrantless search will respect section 8 if authorized by law and both the law and the manner in which the search is conducted are reasonable" (*R*. v. *Feeney* 1997: 155). The Provincial Court held in the *K.B.* case that PCHIP's warrantless search provisions did not satisfy the third criterion, that is, the manner of the search, of the *Feeney* test. In other words, PCHIP could only pass constitutional muster if it provides for some form of show cause hearing where the apprehending authority could be called upon to justify their belief that the child was in serious and imminent danger. Similarly the Provincial Court held that PCHIP's failure to ensure that those affected by apprehensions should have the ability to challenge any apprehension (and not just emergency apprehensions) was unconstitutional because it failed to provide a review mechanism to ensure that the detention was not arbitrary. (Section 10 of the *Charter* contains the right to be free from arbitrary detentions.) The Queen's Bench (federal) decision did not consider either of these issues. It held that, on the facts of the case, neither the warrantless search provisions (as the police officer had obtained consent to enter) nor the pre-authorized apprehension provisions (as this was an emergency apprehension) were engaged, and therefore these issues ought not to have been considered by the lower court.

Thus, the issue of whether PCHIP violates the *Charter's* unreasonable search and seizure protections remains to be decided. However, strong arguments can be made that the act violates these rights unless it provides for a show cause hearing for all apprehensions that were not pre-authorized by a judge.

Places of Detention

When we look at the question of places of detention for apprehended youth, we are once again faced with legal questions regarding the constitutionality of the new legislation. In particular, the meaning of "safe houses" needs to be clarified, and distinguished from "secure care."

Under CFSA models, apprehended children usually are to be taken to a "place of safety." Under PCHIP, apprehended children are to be "confined at a protective safe house" and under the SCA they can be "detained at a secure-care facility." The Manitoba act specifically provides that they cannot be taken to a "detention centre," but PCHIP and SCA do not contain such provisions. The term "safe house" is usually understood by street-level workers and their clients as a drop-in centre, located near where the clients live or work, that provides basic services like meals and showers. Most importantly, this term is used to connote shelters which are "safe from the exercise of someone else's authority" (Lowman 1987: 106). The term "safe house" has been usurped and transformed by PCHIP. The use of "confined" and "detained" indicates that non-consensual detention in locked facilities is authorized by the legislation.

Neither PCHIP or SCA specifically set out the standards for these facilities, rather they are set by provincial regulation. In British Columbia, no SCA regulations have been passed. The Alberta regulations have designated a number of youth centres,[7] including centres which house young offenders and children who have emotional or behavioural disturbances, as "protective safe houses." The Alberta Association of Services for Children and Families has been mandated to set standards for safe houses but they have not done this yet. The PCHIP policy manual (which does not have the force of law) provides that the facilities may be locked and have restricted access and seclusion. All visitors are screened and visits may be supervised. Minors who are subject to a court order can be picked up by the police and returned if they leave the safe house without permission.

The issue of the nature of the facility where apprehended children are held was not considered in the *K.B.* case. While it is beyond the scope of this chapter to review the jurisprudence on the *Charter* rights to liberty of the person and freedom from arbitrary detention, it can be concluded that locked confinement or detention, especially in the absence of clear standards for the facilities (like, for example, how detention is to be enforced against a non-compliant minor) may violate the child's *Charter* rights to liberty and to freedom from arbitrary detention.

Medical Treatment

Do legal minors have the right to refuse medical assessment and treatment? Apprehended street-involved youth are often subject to invasive medical tests and procedures. Here again the question of the constitu-tionality of these interventions is raised, as well as whether this approach helps in the ultimate goal of preventing sexual exploitation of youth.

Unless legislation provides otherwise, the common law "mature minor rule" establishes that a minor who is capable of understanding the nature and consequences of medical treatment and the risks and benefits of receiving or refusing treatment can give legally effective consent (Sneiderman et al. 1995). This rule also permits health-care providers or judges to make determinations regarding the capacity of individual minors to consent to treatment. For example, a court held that a surgeon could make the determination that a "normal, intelligent" sixteen-year-old had sufficient intelligence to understand and therefore consent to an abortion without parental approval (*J.C.S.* v. *Wren*). On the other hand, courts held in the *B.H.* v. *Alberta (Director of Child Welfare)* case, that a sixteen-year-old Jehovah's Witness had, but then lost, the capacity to refuse a blood transfusion; and in the *Chimiliar* v. *Chimiliar* case, that a thirteen-year-old was capable of making a decision whether to receive vaccinations, but that she had lost her capacity to consent. In both of these cases, the children lost capacity because third parties had instilled irrational fears in them.

All traditional CFSAs give welfare authorities the ability to consent to treatment for children in care and some have specific provisions which modify the mature minor rule. For example, the Manitoba CFSA pro-vides that minors sixteen and over who are in care cannot be subjected to a medical examination or treatment without the minor's consent or on a court order. Such orders can only be granted if the child "does not understand relevant information or cannot appreciate the consequences of the decision being made." The Manitoba act makes it clear that the wishes of an informed child must be respected; it does not permit a health care provider to make the assessment of incapacity when the child is over fifteen. Only a court can make this determination.

In contrast, the Alberta act provides that "a child, if the child is capable of forming an opinion, is entitled to an opportunity to express that opinion on matters affecting the child, and the child's opinion should be considered by those making the decisions that affect that child." The Alberta Court of Queen's Bench held in *B.H.* that this section only requires those exercising authority to "consider" but not necessarily "follow" a mature minor's wishes. Child welfare authorities can make the decisions without a court order. In the *B.H.* case the court found that even though a sixteen-year-old Jehovah's Witness had been fully capable of making a decision concerning whether to receive blood products as part of her treatment, her opinion could not be determinative. The court held that it was in her best interests to have the treatment. On appeal, the Alberta Court of Appeal held that the girl had lost the capacity to consent and therefore it was not necessary to decide the issue of whether the statutory provision replaced the mature minor rule.

PCHIP provides that the "director has exclusive custody of the child and is responsible for the child's care, maintenance and well-being while the child is being confined" and that anyone who is apprehended must be "assessed." Regulations passed under PCHIP provide that an assessment of a confined child must include, amongst other things, an assessment of the child's physical health and use of intoxicating substances. These provisions therefore require the director to assess apprehended children and give the director the power to consent to treatment. The PCHIP policy manual states that the "PCHIP worker is responsible for ensuring that an assessment of the child is completed" (*Protection of Children Involved in Prostitution* CF-01-01-06: 6). The SCA clearly states that the director may "authorize" health examinations, "consent to health care if the health care is directly related to the risk that leads to the detainment," and share this information with others including service providers and parents. However, while both PCHIP and SCA give child welfare authorities the ability to consent on a child's behalf, neither of these acts expressly deal with the mature minor rule and therefore it is not clear whether the rule has been displaced or modified. As strong legal arguments can be made both for and against the interpretation that these provisions override the common law rule, it is not clear whether the SCA or PCHIP override the right of mature minors to refuse assessment and treatment. (The issue of consent to medical assessment and treatment was not raised in the *K.B.* case.)

The PCHIP policy manual states that "physical status includ[es] testing for sexually transmitted diseases, HIV, and hepatitis, and pregnancy status" (*Protection of Children Involved in Prostitution* CF-01-01-06: 6). Assessment for drug and alcohol use is also required. Thus, the physical health assessments could include highly invasive tests like drawing blood samples (for alcohol, drug, HIV and hepatitis tests) and gynecological examinations (for STD tests). Justice for Girls, an advocacy group in Vancouver for street-involved girls, has noted the overuse of gynecological examinations for young women in corrections: they call such examinations a sexist form of institutional violence.

If the proper interpretation of PCHIP and SCA is that they override the mature minor rule and permit child welfare authorities to assess and treat minors without their consent, these acts violate the right to security of the person as guaranteed by section 7 the *Charter*. Given the concerns expressed by Justice for Girls, arguments can also be made that non-consensual treatments violate the equality guarantees contained in section 15 of the *Charter*.

Charter violations can be justified on various grounds. In the *B.H.* case (involving the non-consensual use of blood products in the treatment of a sixteen-year-old Jehovah's Witness), the lower court rejected a *Charter* challenge based on security of the person and religious rights. It stated that a child's rights could be overridden in the interests of protecting their "general welfare" (although at another point the court uses the language of "essential treatment" as the basis for *Charter* override justification) as long as the procedures used to make the decision are fair. (The appeal court affirmed the lower court decision on other grounds and held that it was not necessary to decide the *Charter* issues; therefore, the lower court decision in the *B.H.* case is a weak precedent on this issue.) The assessment of girls apprehended under PCHIP will not, in most circumstances, be "essential treatment" although it could be treatment for their "general welfare." If the more stringent "essential treatment" test is the basic standard used to justify the override of *Charter* provisions, and if there is an absence of clear procedures regarding third party consent to the medical assessment and treatment of mature minors, then the PCHIP and SCA provisions on assessment and treatment may indeed violate various *Charter* guaranteed rights of apprehended girls.

Justifications for Charter Violations

This chapter has identified three areas where PCHIP provisions might violate *Charter* rights: failure to provide a review mechanism for all apprehensions and for warrantless searches, failure to set standards for protective safe houses, and the requirement that those apprehended submit to a medical assessment. Section 1 the *Charter* provides that violations of *Charter* rights can be justified (and therefore are acceptable) if the government can establish, first, that it is attempting to address a pressing and substantial problem and, second, that the restriction on the right is proportionate to its objective. This proportionality test considers whether the legislation has a rational connection to the objective it seeks to achieve, minimally impairs the affected rights and strikes a balance between the deleterious and salutary effects of the legislation. While governments could easily establish that exploitation of children through prostitution is a serious and pressing problem, the methods used by the government to address this problem through PCHIP apprehensions may not achieve the outcomes desired and, in fact, may be counter-productive to their realization. Therefore, PCHIP apprehensions may not be proportionate to their objectives. A number of section 1 arguments could be made as to the procedural fairness of the regime and whether the appropriate factors are considered before decisions are made. However, as a full section 1 analysis is beyond the scope of this chapter, only the argument as to whether there is a rationale connection between the PCHIP provisions and what they seek to achieve will be explored.

Four young Albertan woman who participated in a focus group for the Girl Child project were asked what they thought about the secure provisions in PCHIP. In rapid succession, they said the following: "The doors are locked"; "They are going right out on the street again"; "That's going to piss them off"; "Or even better you're going to piss the pimps off"; " That's true"; "They are going to resent people trying to help them"; "You're not helping them.... It's not going to solve anything." This interchange encapsulates some of the ways in which PCHIP may be ineffective and even counter-productive to the objective of getting children out of prostitution.

The apprehensions may not be an effective tool to help girls exit from prostitution, especially since, as the evidence in the *K.B.* case established (*K.B. and M.I. v. Alberta*: para. 35), many of the girls apprehended under PCHIP simply sleep out their time before being released back to the street. Moreover, there is a very serious concern that the possibility of being subjected to secure confinement will impede access to voluntary services.[8] Girls are already distrustful of these services. As one woman stated, "I don't want to go to [a particular service] because they take your picture and give it to the vice squad." The Alberta Task Force on Juvenile Prostitution recognized that "authority figures and those wishing to help (police, social workers, doctors, educators, etc.) are often viewed by youth with scepticism, distrust, and suspicion" (1997: 8). Lost contact with voluntary services means lost opportunities to help street-involved girls to identify and explore other motivations to leave the street, such as pregnancy, burnout or violence. Successful programs need to be in a position to take advantage of the window of opportunity that opens when these situations arise. The fear of apprehension may have the counter-productive effect of driving girls away from voluntary services.

Many of the young women interviewed stated that they preferred to be on the streets rather than hidden in trick pads, massage parlours and hotels. Why?—because that is where their friends are; they are less isolated; they can learn the ropes from each other; they can look out for each other and they know that street services are keeping their eyes open too; they can share information about bad dates; and they can find out about available services. One young woman said about PCHIP,

> You're going to push the prostitutes so far into an isolated area that bad stuff is going to end up happening again. So perhaps that's what is going to happen to these girls, they're going to go out there and the cops won't see them, and then they're going to get screwed up just because of that.

An Alberta service provider echoed this problem stating, "the girls I have worked with since PCHIP has been in place, all of them talk about being driven underground, they are doing more work than ever before." As well, she said,

> I've had a couple of girls who were picked up and taken to safe houses, and those girls got absolutely terrible beatings when they were back on the street because they had been out of circulation, hadn't been making the money they need to make…. Young girls who have left town many more times than they would have normally. They are being circulated a lot more; they're underground.

Thus, it may be that PCHIP pushes young women underground and back to abusive pimps, isolates them and makes it harder for them to escape from sexual exploitation.

Secure confinement regimes can have serious, albeit unintended, counter-productive consequences and therefore may be an ineffective method of protecting girls involved in prostitution. Thus, the argument can be made that the regime cannot be justified as rationally connected to its objective and therefore the government cannot thereby infringe on the *Charter* rights as set out in section 1.

Conclusion

Many policy makers, street workers and researchers are opposed to the use of protective confinement to apprehend minors involved in prostitution. Even those who support such use assert that it should only be employed as a last resort in situations of imminent danger. This last-resort principle is reflected in PCHIP's emergency apprehension provisions but, as I have argued, the principle may be disregarded by the social workers, police, bureaucrats and judges who are responsible for implementing PCHIP. The Supreme Court of Canada has made it clear that governments can pass legislation permitting the apprehension of children in need of protection even in non-emergency situations where there is a serious risk of harm. Governments can take early-intervention measures to prevent harm, as well as to protect against harm. Thus, apprehensions which are not judicially pre-authorized are not *per se* unconstitutional. They are, however, unlawful if the statutory test is not applied by those responsible for the apprehension.

The failure of PCHIP to provide review mechanisms for all apprehension and warrantless search provisions, and to provide standards for protective safe houses, as well as PCHIP's compulsory medical assessment requirement, may violate the constitutional rights of those who are apprehended. Given that the regime may not achieve its objectives, and indeed, may even be antithetical to accomplishing these objectives, these parts of PCHIP may be unconstitutional. In any event the potential negative effects of PCHIP-like regimes are so serious that governments must question whether they will cause more problems than they will solve.

Notes

1. It has been a pleasure to work with the other authors in this collection; their insights over the last two years have significantly influenced my work. I would also like to acknowledge the research assistance of then-law students Laurelle Ajani Harris and Rekha Malaviya early in this project, and the assistance of Colleen Stewart (with the financial assistance of the University of Manitoba Legal Research Institute) as the project drew to a close. The contributions of Muriel St. John, law reference librarian, were, as ever, invaluable.

2. See the British Columbia Ministry for Children and Families, *Report of the Secure Care Working Group*, "Appendix C: Statutes and Programs in Other Canadian Jurisdictions," for a review of secure care provisions in CFSAs.

3. When a pre-apprehension court order is sought, PCHIP requires that the judge be advised whether the child has been apprehended before by court order. (Note that this requirement does not require disclosure of prior emergency applications.) The forms created by the PCHIP regulations do not include a reference to this requirement. Thus, while pre-apprehension orders are rarely sought, those completing the forms probably do not include information on prior apprehensions. There is no requirement that prior apprehensions (either with or without an order) be disclosed at a show cause hearing or a continuing confinement hearing.

4. "Higher threshold" means that PCHIP legislation requires that the risk to the

child must be greater than that which is required for CFSA apprehensions. In particular, the apprehending agent must have information that indicates that the endangerment is serious and imminent. Imminency is not a requirement for CFSA apprehensions.

5. See, for example, Assistant Deputy Ministers' Committee on Prostitution and the Sexual Exploitation of Youth (2000); Provincial Steering Committee on Children and Youth Exploited Through Prostitution (2000); Manitoba Child and Youth Secretariat (1996); Bramly et al. (1998); Kingsley and Mark (2000); First and Second World Congress Against Commercial Sexual Exploitation of Children (1996, 2001); Pellatt (1988); Lowman (1987).

6. As cited in British Columbia Ministry for Children and Family Development (1998, Appendix C, no page).

7. As of March 14, 2002, the following facilities were prescribed by the Protection of Children Involved in Prostitution Regulation (a regulation which is created under authority delegated to PCHIP authorities under the PCHIP Act) as "protective safe houses": Youth Assessment Centre (High Prairie); Youth Assessment Centre (Lac la Biche); Youth Assessment Centre (Red Deer); Yellowhead Youth Centre, Sundance House (Edmonton); Woods Homes (Calgary); Central Peace Group Home (Rycroft); Sifton Children's Centre Protective Safe House (Lethbridge); and Saamis Children's Centre Protective Safe House (Medicine Hat).

8. The feminist interveners in *Winnipeg Child and Family Services* v. *G. (D.F.)* argued interpreting the common law to permit the state to force pregnant women into treatment programs for drug and alcohol abuse during pregnancy would have the effect of driving women away from services. For this reason, the feminist interveners argued, any extension of the law to permit this kind of coercion would violate *Charter* rights and that violation could not be justified. The Supreme Court of Canada did not have to consider the constitutional issues but, in refusing to extend the common law to permit the state to apprehend pregnant women, the court recognized (at para.20) the "danger that the proposed order might impede the goal of healthy infants more than promote it."

Appendix on Provincial Child Protection Statutes

As of April 30, 2002, the following child welfare regimes affecting children involved in prostitution had been enacted or introduced across Canada:

British Columbia: *Secure Care Act* S.B.C.2000, c.28 (not yet proclaimed in force); *Prevention of Child Sexual Exploitation Act* 208/1998 (private member's bill which did not go further than first reading); *Child, Family and Community Services Act* R.S.B.C., 1996, c.46 (as amended 1999, c.26 s.5). The later act specifically states that a child has been or is likely to be sexually abused or sexually exploited if the child has been or is likely to be encouraged or helped to engage in prostitution, or coerced or inveigled into engaging in prostitution.

Alberta: *Protection of Children Involved in Prostitution* 1998, c.P-19 (as amended by 2000 c.P-28); *Children Involved in Prostitution Regulation* A.R. 5/99 (as amended 114/99, 218/99, 37/2001); *Child Welfare Act* R.S.A.2000, c.C-12, s.1(3)(c), s.30(1). Both acts specifically cover children involved in prostitution. In particular, the *Child Welfare Act* s. 1(3)(c) includes "prostitution related activities" as sexual abuse and s.30(1) states that the director may apply for a restraining order if a person has "encouraged or is likely to encourage the child to engage in prostitution."

Saskatchewan: Various PCHIP-like private members bills have been introduced (209/1997, 742/1998, 206/1999 and 2/2002) but none of these bills went further than first reading. *The Child and Family Services Act,* S.S. ch.C-7.2 (as amended 1999, c.14, s.3) specifically includes as a child in need of protection a child who has been exposed or is likely to be exposed to harmful interaction for sexual purposes, including involvement in prostitution.

Manitoba: *The Child and Family Services Act* C.C.S.M. 1985, c.C80. Section 1(c) includes sexual exploitation of the child with or without the child's consent as abuse.

Ontario: *Rescuing Children from Sexual Exploitation Act* Bill 86/01 (a government bill), which passed second reading and was referred to the Standing Committee on Justice and Social Policy, was prorogued on March 2, 2002, and therefore the bill has died. Two other government bills (86/2001;176/2000) and four private members bills (22/2001;10/1999;6/1999;18/1998) have also introduced PCHIP-like legislation but these bills have also died on the order paper. The *Child and Family Services Act* R.S.O.1990, c.C.11(as am. by S.O.1999, c.2, s.9, s.22) now states that a child is in need of protection where the child has been sexually exploited and the person having charge of the child knows or should have known and failed to protect the child, or there is a risk that the child is likely to be sexually exploited. It also creates a duty to report where a child has been sexually exploited or there is a risk that the child is likely to be sexually exploited. This act includes sexually exploited in the definition of "abuse."

Quebec: *Youth Protection Act* R.S.Q. 1977, c.P.34.1. The involvement of children in prostitution is not specifically covered in this legislation.

New Brunswick: *Family Services Act* S.N.B. 1983, c.16, s.31(1)(e) states that a child may be in danger when a child has been "sexually exploited or in danger of such treatment."

Prince Edward Island: *Family and Child Services Act* R.S.P.E.I 1988, c.F–2,s.1(2)(c) states that a child is in need of protection when they have been sexually exploited.

Nova Scotia: *Children and Family Services Act* S.N.S.1990, c.5 does not specifically cover prostitution. *Protection of Children Involved in Prostitution Act*, 117/99, a private member's bill, did not go further than first reading.

Newfoundland: *Child, Youth and Family Services Act* S.N.L. 1998, c.C–12.1. Sections 14(b) and (e) state that a child is in need of protective intervention if the child is being, or is at risk of being, sexually exploited by the child's parent, or is at risk of being sexually exploited by a person and the child's parent does not protect the child.

Yukon: *Children's Act* R.S.Y.1986, c.22. Prostitution is not specifically covered in this legislation.

Nunavut and Northwest Territories: *Child and Family Services Act* S.N.W.T.1997, c.13. Section.7(3) (c) and (d) states that a child needs protection where the child has been sexually exploited by the child's parent or another person, where the child's parent knew or should have known of the possibility of sexual exploitation, or where there is a substantial risk that the child will be sexually exploited and the parent is unwilling or unable to protect the child.

Chapter Six

Balancing Safety, Respect and Choice in Programs for Young Women Involved in Prostitution

Kelly Gorkoff with Meghan Waters

In recent years the issue of youth who are sexually exploited through prostitution has been attracting a great deal of attention: concerted efforts to address the problem have been made globally, nationally, provincially and civically. The purpose of this chapter is to review the Canadian programming response to sexually exploited youth. The data from fifty-four in-depth service provider interviews and information from contact with 170 agencies will be contrasted with the programming experience of forty-five experiential women.

Providing Service: The Big Picture

Providing service and support through programming to girls exploited through prostitution is indeed a difficult one. The key difficulty lies in creating a balance between respecting the need for youths' individualism and independence with the responsibility to provide safety and support. Providing services to youth generally and street youth in particular is difficult (Raychaba 1993; Cauce et al. 1998). Specifically, it is difficult to get youth involved in programming at a time in their lives when they are seeking independence and rejecting authority. Youth often view services and programming with suspicion (Cauce et al. 1998). Classical studies on youth indicate that, generally speaking, youth are in the process of creating identities and searching for independence and autonomy within a societal structure where they do not have legal status and are continually limited by institutions and policy because of their age status (Hall and Jefferson 1976; Coles 1995; Epstein 1998). Indeed, it is often argued that many young people experience estrangement as a result of tension associated with the transition from childhood to adulthood. This difficulty is voiced by some service providers:

> The largest hurdle is to get kids to think they need services, because they think they are invincible.... They are in the invincible stage and that is the way it is ... you know, this is still all fine and dandy, I'll take some condoms but that is all I need from you, don't try and fix my life.

> If someone tells you to do something, especially if you're a teenager, you're more likely to say no.

> Adolescents in terms of accessing resources are often their own worst enemy, they don't have the patience or the skill to work with a system that frustrates them.

When this drive for independence is combined with the multiple needs of street youth, whether in the sex trade or not, the task of providing safety and support becomes that much more difficult. As discussed throughout this book, these youth are dealing with multiple issues such as drug and alcohol use, familial abuse and dysfunction, identity and street-family issues, health and reproduction, cultural pressures, as well as issues of food and shelter. While many service providers see street youth both in and out of the sex trade as victims of child abuse, the youth do not always self-define in that manner, but rather see themselves as empowered and surviving independently. Youth describe themselves as having moved beyond passive beings who can simply be acted on:

> There was constantly people telling me where I needed to go and what I needed to do and, um, trying to lock me up and keep me on probation and all this stuff and when I was on the street, it was like, I had this sense of freedom that I felt I deserved. Like I was fourteen years old but I felt so adult.

Some of the service providers indicated that the issues dealt with by street youth who do not engage in sex-trade work are both similar and different from those that sexually exploited youth confront. The first phase of this study[1] concluded that, in Canada, generic street youth services are more often available than are specific services for sexually exploited girls. Generic programming may suit the needs of some without meeting the needs of all. Because street life and sexual exploitation are so entwined, it is difficult to say which programs work best. Generic services are easily accessible, a place where sexually exploited youth can go to find support for a variety of issues. However, some women suggest that generic services are too encompassing and don't address issues of importance to sexually exploited girls. It appears that those deeply involved in the sex trade find generic services inadequate to meet their needs and often report feeling stigmatized in generic pro-grams. Prostitute-specific services are more likely to be used by those more fully involved in the sex trade. As one woman suggested:

> Well, if it's going to be for prostitutes then it should just be for prostitutes. Just strictly prostitutes. Prostitutes are more comfortable knowing that other prostitutes are there, 'cause I didn't feel comfortable with the number of kids hanging out.

Canadian Service Provision

Since the Badgley Report, Canada has witnessed an increasing and consistent trend among service providers, government and experiential[2] people to regard youth involved in the sex trade as victims of sexual abuse. Almost all of the service providers with whom we spoke noted this:

> These kids have been victimized and exploited. We believe that it is an abuse of children. [It is] the biggest myth going, that this is a lifestyle choice. I think the past five years or so the philosophy has changed that these kids, especially children, even adult prostitutes—but we feel specifically with the kids—that they are the victims out there; we try not to use the word prostitution. We try and use the words sexually exploited and they are victims of abuse.

As discussed in the introduction to this book, Canadian program-ming, almost always made a distinction between youth and adult sex-trade work. Much of this distinction is based on the state-mandated responsibility to protect the rights and safety of children. In Canada, providing for the welfare and safety of those under age eighteen (and, in some provinces, sixteen) is a mandated requirement of the state. Thus, those under age eighteen who are considered to be at risk of harm or engaged in harmful activities are said to be in need of protection and the state has the responsibility to intervene. Consequently, most programs directed toward sexually exploited youth and street youth generally fall under the rubric of caring for those in need of protection, as victims of child abuse, and these services are government mandated.

There are generally three major sources of program delivery for sexually exploited youth in Canada: mandated services, specialized legis-lation and non-governmental services.

Mandated Services

Provincial child welfare agents are mandated to provide service to children deemed to be in need of protection. As discussed in Chapter

Five, there exist many courses of action to be taken to protect children. These include in-home treatment, supervision orders, temporary care or crown wardship.

A high number of youth who engage in sex-trade work have a history of child welfare involvement in their families of origin (Clark and Cooper 2000; Leslie and Hare 2000; Gaetz et al. 1999; Mathews 1989; Raychaba 1993). Sixty-three percent of the women in this study report some type of child welfare involvement. As children, the women were involved for a variety of reasons, such as behaviour problems, and because they were victims of maltreatment including sexual abuse, neglect and parental inability to care for children.

Of those involved with child welfare, the majority indicated they were dissatisfied with child welfare services, as have other such women (Leslie and Hare 2000; Raychaba 1993; Charles and McIntyre 1990; Mathews 1989). Negative experiences include depersonalized care ("I didn't know who my worker was one week to the next"), rigid routines ("like they were telling me what to do, where to go, when to go to bed"), neglect ("they didn't even try to understand what I was going through"), judgmental caregivers ("once they find out you're a prostitute or an addict, they treat you like shit"), unrealistic financial assistance ("eighty dollars a week, while working through all this shit?"), and sexual and physical victimization ("there I was in the room with the guy who raped me"). As some women indicated:

> They are so busy, they have so much stuff to do. What I have found is that they are just running around with their heads cut off, and it's not their fault. It's their workload.... If you talk to somebody for ten minutes, you don't know them, you don't really know what they need.

> When I was in child welfare, you talked. You say stuff to your worker and it goes in one ear and out the other for some of them. They don't really get down to, listen to you.

> I told them [about child sexual abuse] and it was like hard to do. They didn't hear me. They just sent me home.

> I don't believe in counsellors. They never done me no good. They're full of shit. I hate social services. I was raised in social services all my life. I was grown up a very angry, frustrated, neglected child. And that was from this supposedly good people at family services, you know.

In response to negative child welfare experiences, many children run away, finding themselves on the street where they are vulnerable to victimization (see Tyler, Hoyt, Whitbeck and Cauce 2001; Hagan and

McCarthy 1997). Many women indicated that, because they felt blamed for their situation, they were afraid to access services, and so continued to avoid any further contact with child welfare agencies. Many found mandated services to be bureaucratic: they were pushed to sign unrealistic contractual agreements, and finish counselling sessions and programs that did not fit their needs. "I learned to say what they wanted to hear and do what they wanted me to do."

Not all of the participants had child welfare involvement as children. Many became involved with child welfare services in their teens while on the street, having run from home. The women who indicated later involvement also had negative experiences.

> Here's your card, here's your prescription, OK, the cheque's in the mail and your bus pass is in the mail, see you later. That's how they deal with it. They think that if they send you a bus pass and free dental care that everything will be OK. It doesn't work like that. Of course, that's very helpful ... your physical needs are at the top of the list, but you have emotional needs as well. You need emotional stability. They shove kids into school and how can someone concentrate on school when they were just physically abused or whatever? There's a hierarchy of needs—food and shelter first, and then that other stuff.

Most youth suggested that, while shelter and safe houses, or a "decent place to live," was the primary need, it was also the most difficult to access while they were wards of the state. Very often the most important factor related to making a successful transition off the street was a decent place to live (Caputo et al. 1997). In this study, housing was articulated by both service providers and the women as the greatest area of need for girls exploited through prostitution. Without a decent place to live, girls find themselves in a highly vulnerable place, with few options but sex-trade work or sex in exchange for services. As mentioned earlier, one woman told us "If I didn't make money, I had no place to sleep. I had to blow the hotel owner just to get a bed."

The women indicated that there was little support for them between the ages of sixteen and eighteen. (See also Leslie and Hare 2000; Raychaba 1993). Many youth are able to leave the care of the state at sixteen but are faced with other systemic restrictions, like lack of independent housing and ineligibility for social assistance. The situation of these legal minors becomes desperate, leaving them vulnerable to the temptation to work in the sex trade (Novac, Serge, Eberle and Brown 2002). Many on the verge of adulthood fall "through the cracks" or in-between public systems of care—youth care versus social assistance—

because of rules of ineligibility. This point was articulated by one woman who said:

> From sixteen to eighteen there is absolutely nothing. What are you going to do? They [child welfare] are not going to pick you up because you are over the age of sixteen. Your parents don't want to sign you out because they need your welfare cheque. I lived in an abandoned building because I couldn't get any help. The day I turned eighteen, I got everything I needed.

Many child welfare workers with whom we spoke agreed with this reality and often spoke of the difficulties of trying to deal with multiple-need children in an understaffed, highly bureaucratic and underfunded area.

> Right now Child and Family Services has a six- to eight-month waiting list to speak to a counsellor. There has to be safe places for these kids to be [while waiting]. There has to be more family support workers in place.

> The social workers, for the most part, we're seen as the enemy. You know, these kids are afraid of us. Why are they afraid of us? They're afraid of us because traditionally we've taken over their power. You know, we told them we know better than you.

Other service providers indicated that the structure of child welfare doesn't fit the expressed needs and everyday realities of street youth, especially those who are aged sixteen, seventeen and eighteen.

> I cannot presume to make the decisions that they have to make, but I have to provide opportunities so they can make choices. What happens on the street is there is at least the illusion of some choices that they have. Kids who have been in our care and have been abandoned so many times in their life, quite often [the street] gives them back this control.... We [child welfare] need to give them more decisions and opportunities and choices and not make the decisions for them so quickly.

> I guess when I say hostile systems, I am talking about a real lack of willingness to understand or enter into the actual lived experience of people who are on the street who are [surviving] off prostitution. It is more like seeing them automatically as victims that need to be saved and I think that approach makes the system inaccessible. It makes the services inaccessible. It is like you have to take on that victim role to get services because that is what is expected of you. I think that does a real disservice to the actual strengths and smarts that people have.

Although the system intends to provide a positive environment, it appears to have the unintended effect of introducing youth to similarly situated and experienced youth who introduce them to street life as an alternative:

> But what happens quite often in that kind of setting is that it creates other kids saying, you know what, I know how you can survive. What tends to happen is more recruitment in those situations than prevention, so you actually introduce more kids to the street rather than keeping them safe.

It appears that while child welfare protection efforts are designed to support children and youth, the practical experience is often quite different. Listening to the negative experiences of sexually exploited youth and hearing the difficulties of workers in the child welfare system indicates that there are some considerable barriers to success on the part of the child welfare system in assisting girls exploited through prostitution.

Special Legislative Initiatives

Given the inadequacies of the traditional child welfare models to assist youth who are on the street, homeless and involved in the sex trade, many provincial governments have recently explored the option of developing specialized legislation. Alberta was the first Canadian province to pass specific legislation, the *Protection of Children Involved in Prostitution Act* (PCHIP) followed by British Columbia's *Secure Care Act* (SCA) (whose status is currently being reviewed by the government). Legislation similar to PCHIP has also been introduced in Saskatchewan, Nova Scotia, and Ontario, although none of these bills have passed into law. PCHIP is a multifaceted legislation that includes an apprehension component, increased funding for voluntary and non–voluntary services, and the creation of new services specific to children sexually exploited through prostitution. As indicated by a service provider, the philosophy behind those laws is similar to state child welfare responsibility to protect children:

> These are victims of child abuse and sexual predators. The current system isn't working. It's a violent, drug-addicted, poverty-ridden choice where prostitutes are both victims and offenders on a nightly basis and that is the reality of the situation. Yeah, we have to protect people. And no, I don't believe a fourteen-year-old or sixteen-year-old has the mind to say, "I want to go out there and have sex with whoever I want to for the money." There is an onus on police and governments to protect these people until they are able to make choices. Are we punishing kids by locking them up or are they being punished on the street? It's a tough choice.

While several service providers with whom we spoke had been directly impacted by PCHIP legislation in Alberta, only one research participant had used PCHIP services. Therefore, at this time, there really isn't enough information to assess the success or failure of such an approach. However, using the responses of the women and service providers, we have perceptions of success or failure of specialized approaches.

Given the aforementioned difficulties of traditional child welfare models in addressing older youths' issues of street and sex-trade involvement, the majority of service providers with whom we spoke supported the notion of addressing youth prostitution as a specialized problem. Service providers suggested that by separating those who were being exploited from those at risk of exploitation more support could be provided than is normal:

> In the fact that it puts into writing that juvenile prostitution is a form of child sexual abuse, and someone that accesses the services of a prostitute who's under the age of eighteen gets charged with child sexual abuse, I think that's fantastic.

> I think what this bill has allowed us to do is to identify and maintain consistency dealing with the children that have been identified so they don't fall through the cracks—so when child welfare says, we can't do anything, we know she's involved in the streets, but we don't have the time, we can.

However, some service providers argued strongly that specialized approaches, particularly those that employ an apprehension component, were not significantly different from traditional child welfare approaches. In effect they had the result of placing additional constraints on the youth they were trying to help.

While PCHIP and PCHIP-like legislation have numerous components, the most controversial part of the legislation is the apprehension component. Primarily, apprehension has been discussed as a way of protecting young children from abuse in their family of origin, and secure confinement has been viewed as a specially designed way to assist those youth who are severely disturbed, violent to themselves or others, or are otherwise in need of protection (Cauce et al. 1998; Coles 1995). Using apprehension as a tool in assisting youth to leave the street or as a way to protect them from further sexual exploitation through prostitution is indeed controversial. The service providers and women whom we interviewed asked more questions about this approach than they answered. Broadly speaking, the women and service providers suggested that protective confinement would not affect all sex trade-involved youth in the same way. Many service providers and women suggested that many factors other than immediate safety must be taken into account in trying to balance the needs of the youth with the goals of any given "helping" program. These include an individual's past experience with programming, the nature of the confinement model, expectations of the program and level of involvement in the sex trade:

> Like, let's get the kids before they become involved because you have a better chance of helping kids that are at-risk as opposed to kids that are so involved in it that it becomes so much of their lifestyle, it is hard to get them back into the mainstream.

Previous negative experiences with child welfare and police services must be considered in assessing the effectiveness of an apprehension model. One service provider suggested, "You're talking about a group of individuals that have grown up their whole life, have been pro-grammed, you don't trust police, and you don't trust social workers." Thus, the primary consideration is the effect that confining youth will have on their willingness to accept future support. One woman said,

> To lock them up. It's like telling them to shut up and just closing their minds and that.... Kids shouldn't be told to shut up.... They've got to experience good stuff. Locking them up's not the answer. They need to fill minds with positive stuff.

Many service providers agreed. One suggested that confining youth involved in the sex trade has a negative effect for future programming,

> That's automatically putting the kid on guard and, you know, building up a defense mechanism and it, that, the defence mechanism itself is exactly the thing we're trying to get around. Why can't that be done through other avenues other than staying locked up?

Others thought of this model as positive and a potentially helpful way to assist certain types of youth in making contact with service providers and existing programming. Service providers suggested that protective confinement gives a girl a safe place to rest and talk to someone. Others suggested that apprehension might be more effective for youth who did not have a previous negative experience with mandated service or were less entrenched in street life. One PCHIP worker said:

> On the positive side, some of the girls we've worked with, because of our

experience on the streets, we know that in another six to eight months of them being involved on the streets, they'd become quite entrenched. With that entrenchment, you lose bits and parts of your self-esteem—you become so entrenched that you're basically at extreme risk of losing your life. Although we can't prove it, we know a couple of the girls that had become severely entrenched and they are now doing OK but it's our belief that if those women or children hadn't been picked up, some of them would have died in the next five to ten years.

A negative history with child welfare had an impact on women's perceptions of protective confinement models of intervention. The majority of the women who had been apprehended under child welfare legislation were very supportive of voluntary services and suspicious of mandated services. For those who had never been apprehended, there was a greater acceptance of a range of services including involuntary confinement.

Many service providers and women, while not endorsing confinement models, did suggest that if it had to be done, there were key elements that needed to be included: providing a safe environment in which to sleep, eat and clean up; "a safe, safe house ... a place just to get away, you know? A time out. That would be real important"; "no criticism, judgement or authority"; "treat them like humans. Not like pigs or, you know, don't treat 'em like dirt"; and "a worker that is caring, understanding and patient." Many noted that these were the components that women found helpful in many voluntary programs.

Most of the discussion regarding the efficacy of a lockup model focused on two issues: confinement as criminalization and length of confinement. Similar to the literature that suggests protective confinement confuses treatment and punishment (see Lowman 1987; Bittle 2002), many women and service providers asked whether confining youth for prostitution criminalizes the victim:

Are they criminal, or are they victim? If you see it as these individuals being victims of circumstance, then what, if you lock them up, you're sending these kids a mixed message.... You're the victim here, but we're going to lock you up anyway.

It's just more abuse. Like, it's like concentration camps.... What are you going to do with the people you don't want around or the ones you think are uncontrollable or misbehave or don't ... fit in with society? Maybe you can just sort of lock them all up? It never did me a bit of good.

Both the service providers and the women agreed that the current

PCHIP seventy-two-hour confinement is not long enough to accomplish anything positive. Given the complexities of the problem, a limited lockup can do little but provide short-term safety. As one woman advised "Seventy-two-hour lockup is useless, they'll be right back out there after the seventy-two hours." and "It's not long enough to make change in someone's life who's been traumatized from childhood." A service provider suggested:

> You might be keeping a youth or child safe in that lockup, but that's seventy-two hours and then they're back on the street. And if you don't have time to make that connection, and find a way that you can be non-judgmental and build that trust to work with that youth or child. Over the long term, it can be seen, by that child or youth, as just another punishment.... You're not going to fix anything in seventy-two hours.

Moreover others argue that the protective confinement model doesn't take into account the realities of the girls lives. It is important to consider the consequences the youth may face in returning to life on the street after the confinement period. If there has been no real positive connection made to help youth off the street it may be viewed more as punishment than help. A woman said,

> If an underage girl is working for a pimp and you yank her off the street for seventy-two hours and then you let her go and of course, she's gonna go back to her pimp. Hello? Right, she's going to get the beating of her life.

Service providers and some women argued that if a confinement model is used, then it should be long-term and multi-faceted. One woman suggested "Seventy-two hours is not long enough: [the confinement] should be at least six months. We need to physically remove the girls from the environment or else girls will just keep going back."

Although criminalization is usually viewed in a negative way by those experiencing it, involvement in the criminal justice system played a role in their decision to exit:

> I was in a prisoner's box, and they handcuffed me to a bunch of other juvenile girls who were picked up for all kinds of things, whatever. And they handcuffed us and paraded us out, and before court, and this was the most like, this is probably the most intimidating experience of my life, was being in the cells in the court house. They're very small and there's writing on the walls. Like people had scratched in like writings when they've been waiting. And reading all that writing on the walls and thinking about all the people that had been in this room before me. And, I was so scared, and I wanted to be out so badly.

Other women were very clear in their assertion that involvement in apprehension models have a clearly negative impact on youth. They felt most comfortable using voluntary programs. This response seems to indicate that these models are most accepted and approachable and provide the best way to make connections with youth. As one service provider succinctly put it,

> I know that having that place for these kids is much more likely to be successful than locking them up. I absolutely know that and it is like, lock them up till they're eighteen and why do we think we have made a difference? Then they are eighteen and they are on the street—we haven't provided them with the tools to make choices and ways to make themselves safer.

Many service providers wondered whether specialized legislation would be necessary if traditional child welfare agencies were equipped to deal with family issues early on, and at the street level. One service provider lamented, "It's a shame that parents and society have to actually get to the point of locking up the young person to keep them safe. That doesn't make sense."

Indeed, many service providers argued that one of the major gaps nationally is the lack of a child welfare response early on in children's lives. They suggested that child welfare agencies should be focused on providing early support to families, especially those with children at risk, and on creating innovative ways to help children on the street with adequate financial assistance to meet their day-to-day needs.

Both the child welfare and specialized legislation approaches are clearly alike in their argument that sexual exploitation through prostitution is a form of child abuse: preventing youth from engaging in prostitution is their primary focus. These are clearly strategies aimed at protecting youth from abuse. However, almost all of the service providers with whom we spoke, both state and non-state workers, agreed that the issue is a complex one with many areas of overlap. Thus, the approaches to dealing with the issue should differ from traditional child welfare models.

Non-Governmental Programming
There are a large number of Canadian services for street youth, some of which are specific to youth involved in the sex trade, which are independent of governmental mandates. Many of these service providers agreed that providing service to street youth and youth involved in the sex trade was a complex undertaking, requiring a long-term, non-judgmental, empowering approach.

Almost all the non-governmental agencies (NGOs) with whom we spoke have similar goals to mandated and specialized services, including protection from abuse and transition off the street. However, many of these agencies used or advocated methods for reaching those goals that differed from governmental agencies. A growing number of practitioners and researchers endorse service delivery models that stress non-state involvement. These non-state models assume that age shouldn't determine whether one is afforded autonomy in making life choices and decisions to change: they stress collaboration with youth and support their autonomy (Raychaba 1993). Many of these agencies employ a "harms reduction" approach, which focuses on assisting youth to live safely on the street, taking small steps to reduce harm experienced on their way to eventually exiting. This view sees children as both victims and survivors:

> I believe you start by engaging them, by building relationships with them and then offer them things that will help them to get what it is they want, as they discover what it is that they want.

> The sixteen- or seventeen-year-olds, if you go, at least my experience is, you can't make any kid do what they don't want to do but certainly if you give people opportunities then they can make better choices and quite often do. But if you go into a situation with a sixteen- or seventeen-year-old and you say you are prostituting and you can't do that and I won't allow you to do that, you can't be out there, it can, what it can do is tend to be shaming messages, you know what I mean and that is not helpful messages for kids that are being exploited out there. It is really important to provide them with opportunities for safety, for a roof over their head, for food, for those kinds of things and to reel them in rather than think we can just snatch them and lock them up or tell them what to do.

These services included provision of condoms, needle exchanges, bleach kits, street-wise workshops and bad-date sheets.

It is important to note that there is variation in the harms reduction approach. At one end of the scale are programs that regard provision of some of the harms reduction services as enabling: these require youth to no longer be involved in sex-trade work in order to receive services.

> You couldn't be, it would be inappropriate for us to be doing a job training with someone who was still standing on the corner. Um, you know basically you can't use substances while you're here. You can't be intoxicated…. Um…. there's a ten o'clock curfew every night.

On the other end of the harms reduction approach is the advocacy model. This perspective is critical of programs designed to save people from prostitution; it actively advocates for the rights of all sex-trade workers. Although service providers working from this perspective do not directly condone the involvement of youth, they advocate for all workers' rights, health and safety, regardless of age. Their emphasis is on the agency and rights of their client, not imposed protection:

> I find programs that target people to get out of the field offensive. Most programs don't try to help prostitutes, they are services for people or public at large who doesn't want to have this dirty problem of prostitution. How much of this is political in response to morality issues of the right and does not reflect the needs of children. There is a mentality that people have to save the children. Our mission statement is to enable people and provide support and legitimize the work and decriminalize it. We want to assist sex workers in their effort to live and work safely and with dignity. Sex for money is not an inherently disempowering situation to be in. We generally find that when people are ready to move on to something else, they generally do.

I guess it is good to have the whole ethic of saving people from a life in prostitution but for some people there needs to be alternatives to that. Imposing our way of life on people, our liberal attitudes, is wrong. We end up doing more harm than good. An approach in which the experiences and values of people who are actually working the street are incorporated into the systems that are there to serve them is better. Plus, it is clear that NGO approaches to dealing with sexually exploited youth are not solely protectionist strategies but rather employ a variety of program responses to address a variety of needs.

The women with whom we spoke in regard to programming consistently said that they found help through voluntary services. Services used most often by these women included shelters or safe houses, outreach workers' provision of condoms and needles, drug rehabilitation programs, and drop-in centres where they could eat, shower, "hang out" and meet other basic needs. They liked these services because they were staffed by experiential people who were non-judgmental, open and supportive. A number of women spoke in favour of programs run by women for women; as well, the overwhelming majority supported programs with staff who had previous experience on the street.

> Having one-on-one with someone who's been there ... and let them talk with each other because they'll understand more than from someone who reads a book.

Effectiveness? Toward Best Practices

It is clear from the experiences of women and service providers that no single action, policy or program is best for youth exploited through prostitution. Just as there is no standard experience of street entry, there is no typical experience of street exit. Exiting itself is difficult to attain and is often a life-long process. Those women who did leave the sex trade found three main components or themes for programming to be useful. The first was dealing with issues of personal history, primarily childhood abuse. As expressed throughout this volume and elsewhere, familial child abuse and subsequent child welfare involvement consistently precedes sexual exploitation. Those who left the sex trade clearly indicated the need to deal with past abuse. "It's a lifelong thing. And it's, it's just like sometimes I'm exhausted of always trying to live life normally after that."

Second, programming must focus on establishing relationships based on mutual respect, unconditional love and relationship building. One woman spoke highly of her relationship with one worker over numerous years: "[I'd screw up] a lot of times. She was so accepting. I was the first girl she ever had, too. I still talk to her almost every day. Unconditional love. They didn't care how badly I messed up." Many service providers suggested that once a relationship is established, there is greater likelihood that the youth will continue to access the service and trust the workers. One service provider said:

> After a while, once we get to know kids, I mean I can sit here and tear a strip out of a number of kids and yeah, they might, you know, tell me to fuck off and, they'll be back an hour later, because they know that I'm not doing it out of ignorance and knowing I'm not doing it out of just pure spite. They know I'm doing it because I give a shit.

In fact, when asked about factors that might have prevented them from choosing sex-trade work, the women consistently pointed to growing up with stable, loving relationships: "the funny thing is, is most of the time all you want to hear is, 'I love you' from your own parents. That's all, 'I love you, You are worth it'"; "I don't want to sound like no wuss, you know, but I would have liked to have somebody to say nice shit about me, you know?"; "parents that were there or that gave a shit"; "I needed my mother the most, but she was never there and if she was, she didn't really care." Thus, it would seem to follow that a crucial aspect to success in any program, intervention or treatment of youth in care is the development of a secure, stable and consistent relationship with a service provider (see Raychaba 1993; Cauce et al. 1998, Clark and Cooper 2000; Caputo et al. 1997). As Novac, Serge, Eberle and Brown (2002) argue, the isolation and alienation that draw youth to the street is countered by the caring social relations among street youth. Thus, leaving street life obviously requires help with reconnecting socially.

A third component of successful intervention most often mentioned by the women is having control over the transition process. As one young woman put it, "[Program] gives you the chance to change and lets you take as long as you want and they don't force nothing on you. They only encourage you." For another it was, "that kind of atmosphere of kind of self-healing, like, you know what I mean, like doing it at your own pace kind of, I don't know, it just gives you a lot more honour and respect of running your own life kind of thing. Like, that's probably why I'm still off, 'cause this place really has given me a voice. It has given me power."

Service providers also felt that those who leave the street do so because they feel that they have some power and control in the decisions that affect their lives. One stated "People have the right to participate in decisions affecting their lives, it doesn't matter whether you're six years old or whether you are sixty-five years old." Other researchers have noted that homeless street youth are more apt to continue to attend shelters and drop-in centres if they feel they have a stake in the development of the program (Clark and Cooper 2000). Such an empowerment approach is certainly not new. As long ago as 1978, the Report of the Task Force on the Child as Citizen stated:

> While we have developed theories of child development about which there is some agreement, we still embrace these theories from a viewpoint of children being essentially passive and dependent. Their role is to cooperate, obey, and go to school when they are old enough. This attitude sees children, however affectionately, as having no role to play in adult decision making about them. Perhaps innocently, but nonetheless effectively, this perception renders the child invisible. (1978: 81)

Service providers and women alike mentioned numerous service gaps. Housing for youth was seen as the largest service gap. Without housing, women stayed involved in the sex trade so they could make money to pay rent and have a place to sleep. Housing gaps existed at all levels, and included the need for more safe houses, crisis shelters and transitional housing. Many women suggested a model known as "foyer housing" which combines shelter needs with other needs such as training workshops, health and social services, and amenities. Often seen as a "one-stop shopping" model, it is increasingly discussed as a model of support for youth (see Quilgars and Anderson 1997; Ward 1997). The other major gaps mentioned were public education, drug rehabilitation programs specific to youth, and alternative secondary education and employment.

Programming and Funding: Policy Implications[3]

The order in which we have presented service delivery models also reflects funding patterns. Child welfare and specialized legislation programming have the most secure funding because they are built into the baseline budgets of provincial family service departments. NGOs, on the contrary, have the most precarious funding: most depend on short-term, often pilot-project funding and in-house fundraising initiatives. Provincial governments take greater responsibility for programs with a legislative foundation, providing more secure funding to permit the agencies to fulfill their mandate.

At the administrative level the distinction between mandated and non-mandated services is very clear. At the program level, however, these distinctions often become blurred. For example, in Alberta, funding through PCHIP is directed to a number of NGOs that provide a range of voluntary services, while, in other provinces, child welfare agencies may support or fund NGOs providing specific services for children exploited through prostitution. Despite the fact that the boundaries between mandated and non-mandated services may be blurred at the program delivery level, the funding priorities are clearly distinct.

The policy implications of this funding divide are significant. The programs with a legislative foundation, (child welfare and PCHIP) are also tied to an apprehension or protective confinement function regardless of the wishes of the child/youth. From numerous studies (Clark and Cooper 2000; Leslie and Hare 2000; Gaetz et al. 1999; Mathews 1989; Raychaba 1993) and from our own interviews, we know that the majority of children on the street have been involved with the child welfare system. Many of these youth report bad experiences with the child welfare system. From a policy perspective there is a conundrum: the category of children most in need of services are often children suspicious of "controlling" agencies, but these are the very agencies most securely funded to provide the services. Thus, the evolution of securely funded programs with a mandate to protect child sexual abuse victims may have the unintended effect of frightening these children/youth away because of their fear or aversion to the control components of these services.

Non-governmental organizations, on the other hand, have greater degrees of freedom in the provision of services; however, for the most part the cost of that freedom is insecure funding. NGOs that are not tied to a legislative mandate encompass a wide range of services and diverse service philosophies: it appears that insecure funding is their only common denominator.

It is disturbing to find that most of the secure funding tends to be limited to programs with an apprehension or secure-confinement mandate. The one unified message we received from women and service providers alike is that one model does not serve all. Policy makers need to insure that program variety exists; this can best be achieved by providing more secure funding to the NGOs that provide a range of voluntary services on a "harms reduction" and advocacy continuum. These are programs that youth find most accessible and most acceptable.

Piecemeal Solutions?

In discussing youth issues, Epstein (1998) asserts that "institutions view kids and not their situations as the social problem." In other words, we should be careful not to individualize what are essentially social problems. Rather, there is a need for a broader level of analysis. Some of the service providers with whom we spoke suggested that, for every girl who leaves the street, there are two to take her place. The underlying conditions that cause girls to be located in places of vulnerability must be addressed. Looked at this way, youth exploitation through prostitution is clearly a consequence of racism, poverty and sexism, as well as homophobia and ageism. Service providers consistently mentioned poverty as a determinant of youth involvement in the sex trade.

> When kids find themselves in a position of poverty it's very hard for them to claw their way out of it, because in order to survive sometimes they have to go to illegal activities to survive, and then they get wrapped up in the criminal justice system, for example, or in drug use.

Needing to address wider issues of sexism was very often mentioned in the narratives of the women and of the service providers. One service provider suggested that a large hurdle in solving this social problem is posed by the way sexism is embedded in social life, "Our language, media, attitudes about women and children still make it seem that it's OK still." And another said,

> Calvin Klein uses models who look like they're twelve years old and have them lying on a couch and the slogan is "Obsession for Men." I don't care if the model is twenty-five years old, she looks like she's twelve, so that is the image and the message. Half naked on a couch looking like she's in a trick pad or something. How does that eat away at the way we treat women and children?

Each of these factors alone does not cause sexual exploitation of girls. The intersection of poverty with the devaluation of women, previously experienced violence, marginalization and the ease with which prostitution is made available as an alternative contribute to the sexual exploitation of girls through prostitution.

Conclusion

Generally, in Canada, street youth are managed through standardized state policies administered by the criminal justice and social service systems. It is crucial to note that these response systems do not always appear to be successful in the long term, and they often have unintended effects, such as alienating youth. Although the women in this study limited their involvement in state services, seeing them as a form of control, not assistance, they had been a dominant force throughout much of their childhood and youth years. The women advocated for safe houses and voluntary programs. Safety in their minds moved beyond physical safety to include safety from child welfare agents and police.

Another important concern which needs to be addressed is the level of entwinement of issues of youth sex-trade work with those of street youth generally. While separating these issues may be helpful for assisting youth, it may also have the unintended effect of labelling and stigmatizing youth: once sex-trade involvement becomes associated with one's identity, it provides a stronger pull to street life. Further, the additional separation of youth sex trade involvement from advocacy approaches of adult prostitution may also leave youth unsupported and in a position of vulnerability to state responses. The advocacy movement must address youth work more strongly than it presently does.

It is clear that treating youth involved in prostitution solely as victims of abuse has limited usefulness. Phoenix (2002) argues that, by casting young people as victims, the generalities of their lives are subsumed by the notion of their victimhood. She further argues that the consequence of the victim label is an erasure of the social and material uniqueness of being a young person involved in prostitution: all the relevant issues of prostitution, such as health and safety, stigma and working conditions, are silenced, because the victim label has supremacy. This removes a sense of agency from the youth, their choices and their lives, and largely ignores the material and social context in which the decision to prostitute is made. To eradicate the inequities and exploitation associated with youth prostitution, it is necessary to take into account broader social issues. The experiences reflected throughout this book strongly suggest that more attention needs to be given to the social structures, such as poverty, that exist beyond, yet give rise to, prostitution. It is instructive to link prostitution to broader issues such as the economic and political marginalization of youth and the inequities of gender relations. Youth occupy a different position in society vis-á-vis adults—they are unemployed at higher rates, occupy marginal labour-force positions, are targets of capital in different ways than adults and have little political power and citizenship (see Allahar and Côté 1998). As Hollands (forthcoming 2003) argues, there is a need in Canada to analyze the relationship between a particular socially constructed age-stage, an economic mode of production and reproduction (capitalist patriarchy) and the socio-spatial and cultural forms of life this combination engenders. Theorizing about youth this way will illuminate issues of youth prostitution. For youth prostitution to be eradicated and youth to be saved from such exploitation, their marginal position needs to be recognized and dealt with. Some have argued that it is necessary to provide youth a living wage to compensate for this marginal position. As well, prostitution as it currently exists implicates women differently than men. This, along with labour-force segregation for women and the sexualization of women's bodies, also needs to be addressed. The gendered nature of sex work, male power to purchase sex, and the often exploitive nature of sex work are all issues that must be addressed. There must also be a recognition of how these issues uniquely impact young women. Feminist concerns must bridge with concerns of youth, particularly young women.

Within this framework, one can argue that it is not the girls that need to be fixed, but rather the material conditions that give rise to the choice to prostitute and the governments that are mandated to service and protect the best interests of the girl child. This requires some innovation on the part of those institutions to understand that the decision to engage in sex work by youth goes beyond issues of victimization into issues of social and economic marginalization. Given that, to date, the strategies to address youth in the sex trade have not addressed a social-change perspective, they appear as little more than Band-Aid solutions.

Notes

1. The research reported in this volume is the second phase of a multiphased research project. The first phase focused on the state of the girl child in Canada and compiled a national inventory of programs available for the girl child.
2. "Experiential" people are those who had former experience in the sex trade.
3. This section is adapted from Busby, Downe, Gorkoff, Nixon, Tutty and Ursel 2002.

References

Abrams, L.S., and L. Curran. 2000. "Wayward Girls and Virtuous Women: Social Workers and Female Delinquency." Volume 15 Affilia: *Journal of Women and Social Work* 49–65.

Adelson, N. 2000. *"Being Alive Well": Health and the Politics of Cree Well-Being.* Toronto, ON: University of Toronto Press.

Alberta Task Force on Juvenile Prostitution (The Forsyth Report). 1997. *Children Involved in Prostitution.* Edmonton, AB: Ministry of Alberta Family and Social Services.

Allahar, A., and J. Côté. 1998. *Richer and Poorer: The Structure of Inequality in Canada.* Toronto, ON: Lorimer.

Alliance of Five Research Centres on Violence. 1999. *Violence Prevention and the Girl Child: Final Report.* London, ON: Alliance of Five Research Centres on Violence.

Arnold, E.M., J.C. Steward and C.A. McNeece. 2000. "The Psychosocial Treatment Needs of Street-walking Prostitutes: Perspectives From a Case Management Approach." *Journal of Offender Rehabilitation* 30(3–4): 117–32.

Assistant Deputy Ministers Committee on Prostitution and the Sexual Exploitation of Youth. 2000. *Sexual Exploitation of Youth in British Columbia.* Vancouver, BC: Ministry of the Attorney General.

Backhouse, C. 1984. "Canadian Prostitution Law 1839–1972." In *Prostitution in Canada.* Ottawa, ON: Canadian Advisory Council on the Status of Women.

Badgley, R. (Chairman). 1984. *Sexual Offences Against Children. Volume 1: Report of the Committee on Sexual Offences Against Children and Youths.* Ottawa, ON: Ministry of Supply and Services.

Bagley, C., and L. Young. 1987. "Juvenile Prostitution and Child Sexual Abuse: A Controlled Study." *Canadian Journal of Community Mental Health*, 6(1):5–26

Barnard, M. 1993. "Violence and Vulnerability: Conditions of Work for Street-Working Prostitutes." *Sociology of Health and Illness* 15: 682–705.

Barry, K. 1984. *Female Sexual Slavery.* New York, NY: Avon.

Benoit, C., and A. Millar. 2001. *Dispelling Myths and Understanding Realities: Working Conditions, Health Status, and Exiting Experiences of Sex Workers.* Victoria, BC.: Prostitutes Empowerment, Education and Resource Society (PEERS).

Berman, H., and Y. Jiwani (eds). 2002. *In The Best Intehnn bmrests of the Girl Child: Phase II Report.* London, ON: The Alliance of Five Research Centres on

Violence.

Biehal, N., and J. Wade. 1999. "Taking a Chance? The Risk Associated with Going Missing from Substitute Care." *Child Abuse Review* 8(6): 366–76.

Bittle, S. 2002. "When Protection is Punishment: Neo-liberalism and Secure Care Approaches to Youth Prostitution." *Canadian Journal of Criminology*. July 2002: 317–50.

Border, B. 2000. "Is There Justice for Girls?" Presentation at the 13th Annual National Association of Women and the Law Conference. Calgary, AB: May 6.

Boyd, S. 1999. *Mothers and Illicit Drugs: Transcending the Myths*. Toronto: University of Toronto Press.

Bramly, L., M. Tubman and Summit Rapporteurs. 1998. *Final Report - Out from the Shadows: International Summit of Sexually Exploited Youth*. Out From the Shadows and Into the Light: The Sexually Exploited Youth Project. Vancouver, BC: Save the Children Canada.

Brannigan, A., and J. Fleischman. 1989. "Juvenile Prostitution and Mental Health: Policing Delinquency or Treating Pathology." *Canadian Journal of Law and Society* 4:77–98.

Brannigan, A., L. Knafla and C. Levy. 1989. *Street Prostitution: Assessing the Impact of the Law, Calgary, Regina and Winnipeg*. Ottawa, ON: Department of Justice.

Brannigan, A., and E.G. Van Brunschot. 1997. "Youthful Prostitution and Child Sexual Trauma." *International Journal of Law and Psychiatry* 20(3):337–54.

Brewis J and S. Linstead. 2000. "The Worst Thing is the Screwing": Consumption and the Management of Identity in Sex Work. *Gender, Work and Organization* 7:84–96.

British Columbia Ministry for Children and Family Development. 1998. "Report of the Secure Care Working Group." Available at <http://www.cf.gov.bc.ca/secure_care/secure_care_report/securecare_4.htm>.

Brock, D. 1998. *Making Work, Making Trouble: Prostitution as a Social Problem*. Toronto, ON: University of Toronto Press.

Brock, R.N., and S.B. Thistlehwaite. 1996. *Casting Stones: Prostitution and Liberation in Asia and the United States*. Minneapolis: Augsburg Fortress.

Brussa, L. 1998. "The TAMPEP Project in Western Europe." In K. Kempadoo and J. Doezema (eds.), *Global Sex Workers: Rights, Resistance and Redefinition*. London, UK: Routledge.

Bruton, J.G. 2000. *Canadian Attitudes About Children in the Sex Trade*. Vancouver, BC: Save the Children Canada.

Busby, K., P. Downe, K. Gatkoff, K. Nixon, L. Tutty and J. Ursel. 2002. "Examination of Innovative Programming for Children and Youth Involved in Prostitution." In H. Berman and Y. Jiwani (eds.), *In the Best Interests of the Girl Child: Phase II Report*. London, ON: The Alliance of Five Research Centres on Violence.

Campagna, D., and D. Poffenberger. 1988. *The Sexual Trafficking in Children: An*

Investigation of the Child Sex Trade. Dover, MA: Auburn House.

Campbell, N. 2000. *Using Women: Gender, Drug Policy and Social Justice.* London, UK: Routledge.

Caputo, T., R. Weiler and J. Anderson. 1997. *The Street Lifestyle Study.* Ottawa, ON: Ministry of Public Works and Government Services Canada.

Caputo, T., R. Weiler and K. Kelly. 1994. *Phase II of the Runaways and Street Youth Project: The Ottawa Case Study.* Ottawa, ON: Ministry of Supply and Services Canada.

Cauce, A.M., E. Embry, L. Morgan, T. Lohr and W. Heger. 1998. "Homeless Youth in Seattle." In K. Kutash, A. Duchnowski and M. Epstein (eds.), *Community Based Programming for Children with Serious Emotional Disturbances: Research and Evaluation.* Baltimore, MD: Brookes Publishing.

Charles, G., and S. McIntyre. 1990. *The Best of Care.* Ottawa, ON: Canadian Child Welfare Association.

Chesney-Lind, M., and R. Shelden. 1992. *Girls, Delinquency, and Juvenile Justice.* Pacific Grove, CA: Brooks/Cole.

Clark, M., and M. Cooper. 2000. *Homeless Youth: Falling Between the Cracks: An Investigation of Youth Homelessness in Calgary.* Calgary, AB: Youth Alternative Housing Committee.

Coles, B. 1995. *Youth and Social Policy.* London, UK: UCL Press.

Cusick, L. 2002. "Youth Prostitution: A Literature Review." *Child Abuse Review.* 11: 230–50.

Dalla, R.L. 2000. "Exposing the Pretty Woman Myth: A Qualitative Examination of the Lives of Female Streetwalking Prostitutes." *The Journal of Sex Research* 37: 344–53.

_____. 2001. "Et tu Brute? A Qualitative Analysis of Streetwalking Prostitute's Interpersonal Support Networks." *Journal of Family Issues* 22(8):1066–85.

_____. 2002. "Night Moves: A Qualitative Investigation of Street-level Sex Work." *Psychology of Women Quarterly* 26(1):63–73.

Dawson, R. 1987. "Child Sexual Abuse, Juvenile Prostitution and Child Pornography: The Federal Response." *Journal of Child Care* 3(2):19–51.

Department of Justice. 1989. *Street Prostitution: Assessing the Impact of the Law: Synthesis Report.* Ottawa, ON: Research Section, Department of Justice.

Desjarlais, V. 1994. *Written Presentation for Forum on Youth Prostitution.* Regina, SK: Street Workers Advocacy Project.

Diduck, A., and W. William Wilson. 1997. "Prostitutes and Persons." *Journal of Law and Society* 24(4):504–29.

Downe, P.J. 1997. "Constructing a Complex of Contagion: The Perceptions of AIDS Among Working Prostitutes in Costa Rica." *Social Science and Medicine* 44(10):1575–1583.

_____. 1998. "Selling Sex, Studying Sexuality: Voices of Costa Rican Prostitutes and Visions of Feminists." *Atlantis* 23(1):60–67.

_____. 2001. "Playing with Names: How Children Create Identities of Self in Anthropological Research." *Anthropologica* 63(2):165–77.

Duchesne, D. 1997. "Street Prostitution in Canada." *Juristat Service Bulletin* 17(2): 1–19. Ottawa, ON: Canadian Centre for Justice Statistics.

Dworkin, A. 1988. *Pornography: Men Possessing Women.* New York, NY, Penguin

Epele, M.E. 2002. "Gender, Violence and HIV: Women's Survival in the Streets." *Culture, Medicine and Psychiatry* 26(1):33–54.

Epstein, J.S. 1998. "Introduction: Generation X, Youth Culture and Identity." In Epstein (ed.), *Youth Culture: Identity in a Post Modern World.* Malden, MA: Blackwell.

Estes, R. 2001. *The Commercial Sexual Exploitation of Children in the U.S., Canada and Mexico.* Available at <www.caster.ssw.upenn.edu/~restes/CSEC.htm>.

Farley, M., I. Baral, M. Kiremire and U. Sezgin. 1998. "Prostitution in Five Countries: Violence and Post-Traumatic Stress Disorder." *Feminism and Psychology* 8(4):405–26.

Farley, M., and H. Barkan. 1998. "Prostitution, Violence Against Women, and Post-Ttraumatic Stress Disorder." *Women and Health* 27:37–49.

Farmer, P. 1999. *Infections and Inequalities: The Modern Plagues.* Berkeley, CA: University of California Press.

Federal-Provincial-Territorial Working Group on Prostitution. 1998. *Report and Recommendations in Respect of Legislation, Policy and Practices Concerning Prostitution-Related Activities.* Ottawa, ON: Department of Justice.

Fillmore, C., C.A. Dell and the Elizabeth Fry Society of Manitoba. 2000. *Prairie Women, Violence, and Self-harm.* Winnipeg, MB: Elizabeth Fry Society.

First Call. 1996. *An Overview of Child and Youth Issues in British Columbia.* Vancouver, BC: First Call.

First World Congress Against Commercial Sexual Exploitation of Children. 1996. *Declaration and Agenda for Action.* Available from <http://www.csecworldcongress.org/PDF/en/Stockholm/Outome_documents/Stockholm%20Declaration%201996_EN.pdf>.

Fisher, G.L., and T.C. Harrison. 1997. *Substance Abuse: Information for School Counsellors, Social Workers, Therapists, and Counsellors.* London, UK: Allyn and Bacon.

Foa, E.B., B.O. Rothbaum, D.S. Riggs and T. Murdoch. 1991. "Treatment of Post-Traumatic Stress Disorder in Rape Victims: A Comparison Between Cognitive Behavioral Procedures and Counselling." *Journal of Consulting and Clinical Psychology* 59:715–23.

Fraser, P. (Chair). 1985. *Pornography and Prostitution in Canada: Report of the Special Committee on Pornography and Prostitution.* Ottawa, ON: Ministry of Justice and Attorney-General of Canada.

Gaetz, D., B. O'Grady and B. Vaillancourt. 1999. *Making Money: The Shout Clinic Report on Homeless Youth and Unemployment.* Toronto, ON: Central Toronto Community Health Centres.

Gemme, R. 1987. *Proceedings of the National Consultation on Adolescent Prostitution.* Ottawa, ON: Canadian Child Welfare Association (CCWA).

Gemme, R., A. Murphy, M. Bourque, M.A. Nemeh and N. Payment. 1984. "A Report on Prostitution in Quebec." *Working Papers on Prostitution and Pornography, Report No. 11.* Ottawa, ON: Department of Justice.

Guinan, M., and A. Hardy. 1987. "Epidemiology of AIDS in Women in the United States, 1981–1986." *Journal of the American Medical Association* 257:2039–43.

Hagan, J., and B. McCarthy. 1997. *Mean Streets: Youth Crime and Homelessness.* Cambridge, MA: Cambridge University Press.

Hall, S., and T. Jefferson. 1976. *Resistance through Rituals.* London: Hutchinson.

Hartmann, H. 1981. "The Unhappy Marriage of Marxism and Feminism: Towards a More Progressive Union." In L. Sargent (ed.), *Women and Revolution: A Discussion of the Unhappy Marriage of Marxism and Feminism.* London, UK: Pluto Press.

Health Canada. 2002. "HIV and AIDS among Youth in Canada." *HIV/AIDS Epi Update.* Ottawa, ON: Health Canada.

Hedmann, P., and Steering Committee Members. 1998. *Strategic Action Plan: Stolen Innocence: A National Education Campaign Against the Commercial Sexual Exploitation of Children.* Toronto, ON: ECKPAT-Canada February.

Heinrich, Jeff. 1995. "Law fails to protect child prostitutes, experts charge." *Calgary Herald*, August 30.

Hekman, S. 1995. "Subjects and Agents: The Question for Feminism." In J. Kegan Gardiner (ed.), *Provoking Agents: Gender and Agency in Theory and Practice.* Chicago, IL: University of Illinois Press.

Hollands, R. 2003 (forthcoming). "Towards a Political Economy of Canadian Youth." In W. Clement and L. Vosko (eds.), *Changing Canada: Political Economy as Transformation.* Montreal: McGill-Queen's University Press.

Hoyt, Dan R., R.D. Ryan and Ana Mari Cauce. 1999. "Personal Victimization in a High Risk Environment." *Journal of Research in Crime and Delinquency* 36:371–92.

Inciardi, J.A., D. Lockwood and A.E. Pottieger. 1993. *Women and Crack-Cocaine.* Toronto, ON: Maxwell Macmillan Canada.

Jackson, L., and A. Highcrest. 1996. "Female Prostitutes in North America: What are Their Risks of HIV Infection.?" In L. Hankins and L. Bennett (eds.), *AIDS as a Gender Issue: Psycho-Social Perspectives.* London, UK: Taylor and Frances.

James, C., and A.Shadd (eds.). 2001. *Talking about Identity: Encounters in Race, Ethnicity and Language.* Toronto, ON: Between the Lines.

Janus, M., A. McCormack, A.W. Burgess and C. Hartman. 1987. *Adolescent Runaways: Causes and Consequences.* Lexington, MA: Lexington Books.

Jiwani, Y. 1998. "Trafficking and Sexual Exploitation of Girls and Young Women: A Review of Select Literature and Initiatives." Vancouver, BC: FREDA Centre for Research on Violence against Women and Children.

Joseph, C. 1995. "Scarlet Wounding: Issues of Child Prostitution." *Journal of Psycho History* 23(1):2–17.

Justice for Girls. 2001. "Statement of Opposition to the *Secure Care Act.*"Available from <www.justiceforgirls.org/publications/pos_securecareact.html>.

Kempadoo K., and J. Doezema (eds.). 1998. *Global Sex Workers: Rights, Resistance and Redefinition.* London, UK: Routledge

Kingsley, C., and M. Mark. 2000. *Sacred Lives: Canadian Aboriginal Children and Youth Speak Out about Sexual Exploitation.* National Aboriginal Consultation Project. Vancouver, BC: Save the Children Canada.

Koshan, Jennifer, together with staff and volunteers from the Elizabeth Fry Society of Calgary. 2001. "Alberta (DIS)Advantage: *The Protection of Children Involved in Prostitution Act* and the Rights of Young Women." Presentation at Women's Resistance: From Victimization to Criminalization Conference. Ottawa, ON, October 1.

Lau, E. 1989. *Runaway: Diary of a Street Kid.* Toronto, ON: Harper and Collins.

Lefler, J. 1999. "Shining the Spotlight on Johns: Moving Toward Equal Treatment of Male Customers and Female Prostitutes." *Hastings Women's Law Journal* 10(1): 11–35.

Leslie, B., and F. Hare. 2000. *Improving the Outcomes for Youth in Transition from Care.* Toronto, ON: Toronto Working Group of the Children's Aid Society of Toronto, Covenant House and Ryerson University Research Project, 1995–1999.

Lock, M., and N. Scheper-Hughes. 1990. "A Critical-Interpretive Approach in Medical Anthropology: Rituals and Routines of Discipline and Dissent." In T. Johnson and C. Sargent (erds.), *Medical Anthropology: A Handbook of Theory and Method.* New York, NY: Greenwood.

Loken, G. 1987. "Child Prostitution." In *National Center for Missing and Exploited Children, Child Pornography and Prostitution: Background and Legal Analysis.* Washington, DC: U.S. Department of Justice.

Lowman, J. 1987. "Taking Young Prostitutes Seriously." *Canadian Review of Sociology and Anthropology* 24(1):99–116.

_____. 1998. "Prostitution Law Reform in Canada." In Institute of Comparative Law in Japan, *Toward Comparative Law in the 21st Century.* Tokyo, Japan: Chuo University Press.

_____. 2000. "Violence and the Outlaw Status of (Street) Prostitution." *Violence Against Women* 6(9):987–1011.

Lowman, J., and L. Fraser. 1995. *Violence Against Persons who Prostitute: The Experience in British Columbia.* Ottawa, ON: Department of Justice Canada.

Lynne, Jackie. 1998. *Colonialism and Sexual Exploitation of Canadian First Nation Women.* Presented at the American Psychological Association, San Francisco, CA, August 17.

Lyon, M., and J. Barbalet. 1994. "Society's Body: Emotion and Somatization of Social Theory." In T. Csordas (ed.), *Embodiment and Experience: The Existential Ground of Culture and Self.* Cambridge, MA: Cambridge University Press.

MacKinnon, C. 1987. *Feminism Unmodified: Discourses on Life and Law.* Cambridge, MA: Harvard University Press.

Manitoba Child and Youth Secretariat. 1996. *Report of the Working Group on Juvenile Prostitution*. Winnipeg, MB: Manitoba Child and Youth Secretariat.

Marquez, P.C. 1999. *The Street is My Home: Youth and Violence in Caracas*. Stanford, CA: Stanford University Press.

Mathews, F. 1989. *Familiar Strangers: A Study of Adolescent Prostitution*. Toronto, ON: Central Toronto Youth Services.

McCarthy, B. 1995. *On The Streets. Youth in Vancouver*. Vancouver, BC: Research Evaluation and Statistics Branch, Ministry of Social Services.

McCormack, J., and J. Burgess. 1986. "Runaway Youths and Sexual Victimization: Gender Differences in Adolescent Runaway Population." *Child Abuse and Neglect* 10:387–95.

McElroy, W. 1997. *A Feminist Defense of Pornography*. Available from <www.freeinquirynetwork.com/FeministDefense.html>.

———. 1998. *The Reasonable Woman*. Boston, MA: Prometheus Books.

McEvoy, M., and J. Daniluk. 1995. "Wounds to the Soul: The Experiences of Aboriginal Women as Survivors of Sexual Abuse." *Canadian Psychology* 36:221–35.

McIntyre, S. 1999. "The Youngest Profession: The Oldest Oppression: A Study of Sex Work." In C. Bagley and K. Mallick (eds.), *Child Sexual Abuse and Adult Offenders: New Theory and Research*. Aldershot, UK: Ashgate.

McMullen, R.J. 1987. "Youth Prostitution: A Balance of Power." *Journal of Adolescence* 10: 35–43.

McNay, L. 2000. *Gender and Agency: Reconfiguring the Subject in Feminist Social Theory*. New York, NY: Polity.

Miki, E. 1995. "Foreign Women in Japan: Victims of Slavery." *Asian Migrant* 8(1): 20–23.

Miller, C.L., M. Tyndall, P. Spittal, K. Li, N. Laliberté and M.T. Scheter. 2002. "HIV Incidence and Associated Risk Factors Among Young Injection Users." AIDS 16(3):491–93.

Miller, J. 1993. "Your Life is on the Line Every Night You're on the Streets: Victimization and Resistance Among Street Prostitutes." *Humanity and Society* 17:422–46.

Miller, J., and M. Schwartz. 1995. "Rape Myths and Violence Against Street Prostitutes." *Deviant Behaviour* 16:1–23.

Morris, D. 1998. *Illness and Culture in the Postmodern Age*. Berkeley, CA: University of California Press.

Nadon, S., C. Koverola and E. Schludermann. 1998. "Antecedents to Prostitution: Childhood Victimization." *Journal of Interpersonal Violence* 13:206–21.

National Center for Missing and Exploited Children. 1992. *Female Juvenile Prostitution: Problem and Response*. Washington, DC: National Center for Missing and Exploited Children.

———. 1998. *Child Prostitution*: Washington, DC: National Center for Missing and Exploited Children.

Nixon, K., L. Tutty, P. Downe, K. Gorkoff and J. Ursel. 2002. "The Everyday Occurrence: Violence in the Lives of Girls Exploited through Prostitution." *Violence Against Women* 8:1016–43.

Novac, S., L. Serge, M. Eberle and J. Brown. 2002. *On Her Own: Young Women and Homelessness in Canada*. Ottawa, ON: Status of Women Canada. Available from <http://www.swc-cfc.gc.ca>.

O'Neill, M. 2001. *Prostitutes and Feminism: Towards a Politics of Feeling*. Oxford, UK: Polity.

Pellatt, A. 1988. "Juvenile Prostitution: A Consideration of the Child Welfare Response." Edmonton, AB: [Alberta] Legislative Planning.

Phoenix, J. 1998. "Prostitutes, Ponces, and Poncing: Narratives of Violence." In P. Bogguley and J. Seymour (eds.), *Relating Intimacies: Power and Resistance*. Basingstoke, UK: Macmillan.

———. 2002. "In the Name of Protection: Youth Prostitution Policy Reforms in England and Wales." *Critical Social Policy*. 22(2):353–75.

Protection of Children Involved in Prostitution, Cf-01-01-06. Internal Procedures Manual for PChIP Staff. Edmonton: Alberta Children's Services.

Provincial [Manitoba] Steering Committee on Children and Youth Exploited Through Prostitution. 2000. *Report and Recommendations*. Winnipeg, MB.

Pyett, P., and D. Warr. 1999. "Women at Risk in Sex Work: Strategies for Survival." *Journal of Sociology* 35:183–97.

Quilgars, D., and I. Anderson. 1997. "Addressing the Problem of Youth Homelessness and Unemployment: The Contribution of Foyers." In R. Burrows, N. Pleace and D. Quilgars (eds.), *Homelessness and Social Policy*. London, UK: Routledge.

Raychaba, B. 1993. *Pain, Lots of Pain: Family Violence in the Lives of Young People in Care*. Ottawa, ON: National Youth in Care Network.

Raymond, J. 2001. "Health Effects of Prostitution." In Donna Hughes (ed.), *Making the Harm Visible: Global Sexual Exploitation of Women and Girls: Speaking Out and Providing Services*. Available at <http://www.uri.edu/artsci/wms/hughes/mhvhealt.htm>.

Ridge, D., V. Minichiello and D. Plummer. 1997. "Queer Connections: Community, 'The Scene' and an Epidemic." *Journal of Contemporary Ethnography* 26:146–81.

Roeters, K. 1987. *From the Other Side: Final Report from the National Juvenile Prostitution Survey*. Ottawa, ON: National Youth in Care Network.

Royal Commission on Aboriginal Peoples. 1996. *Gathering Strength (Volume 3)*. Report of the Royal Commission on Aboriginal Peoples. Ottawa, ON: Canadian Communications Group.

Save the Children Canada. 2000. *Leaving the Streets: Youth Forum to Address the Sexual Exploitation of Children*. Vancouver, BC: Save the Children Canada.

Schissel, B., and K. Fedec. 1999. "The Selling of Innocence: The Gestalt of Danger in the Lives of Youth Prostitutes." *Canadian Journal of Criminology* 41:33–56.

Scott, S. 1998. *Attractions and Aversions: Exploring Attitudes and Perceptions of Sexually Procured Youth in the Downtown Eastside.* Masters Thesis, School of Social Work, University of British Columbia, Vancouver, BC.

Second World Congress Against Commercial Sexual Exploitation of Children. 2001. Outcome Documents. Available from <http://www.unicef.org/events/yokohama/outcome.html>.

Shaver, F. 1996. "The Regulation of Prostitution: Setting the Morality Trap." In B. Schissel and L. Mahood (eds.), *Social Control in Canada.* Scarborough, ON: Prentice Hall.

Silbert, M.H., and A.M. Pines. 1981. "Sexual Child Abuse as an Antecedent to Prostitution." *Child Abuse and Neglect* 5:407–11.

Sneiderman, B., J. Irvine and P. Osborne. 1995. *Canadian Medical Law: An Introduction for Physicians, Nurses and Other Health Care Professionals* (second edition). Toronto, ON: Carswells.

Special Committee to Prevent the Abuse and Exploitation of Children Through the Sex Trade. 2001. *Final Report to the Legislative Assembly of Saskatchewan.* Saskatoon, SK.

Statistics Canada. 2000. *Women in Canada 2000: A Gender-Based Statistical Report.* Ottawa, ON: Statistics Canada.

Strange, C., and T. Loo. 1997. *Making Good: Law and Moral Regulation in Canada, 1967–1939.* Toronto, ON: University of Toronto Press.

Street Workers Advocacy Project. 1996. *Final Report.* Regina, SK: The Council on Social Development Regina Inc.

Sullivan, T. 1986. "The Politics of Juvenile Prostitution." In Lowman and Fraser (eds), *Regulating Sex: An Anthology of Commentaries on the Findings and Recommendations of the Badgley and Fraser Reports.* Vancouver, BC, Simon Fraser University Press.

_____. 1988. "Juvenile Prostitution: A Critical Perspective." In F.E. Hagan and M.B. Sussman (eds.), *Deviance and the Family.* London, UK: Haworth Press.

Sztompka, P. 1994. *Agency and Structure: Reorienting Social Theory.* Yverdon, Switzerland, Langhorne, PA: Gordon and Breech Science.

Task Force on the Child as Citizen. 1978. *Admittance Restricted: The Child as Citizen in Canada.* Ottawa, ON: Canadian Council on Children and Youth.

Thibodeau, P. (ed.). 1996. *Egadz Year End Report.* Saskatoon, SK: Downtown Youth Centre.

Treichler, P.A. 1988. "AIDS, Gender, and Biomedical Discourse: Current Measures for Meaning." In E. Fee and D. Fox (eds.), *AIDS: The Burdens Of History.* Berkeley, CA: University of California Press.

Tutty, L. 1998. "Mental Health Issues of Abused Women: The Perceptions of Shelter Workers." *Canadian Journal of Community Mental Health* 17(1):79–102.

Tyler, K.A., L.B. Whitbeck, D.R. Hoyt and A.M. Cauce. 2001. "The Impact of Childhood Sexual Abuse on Later Sexual Victimization Among Runaway Youth." *Journal of Research on Adolescence* 11(2):151–76.

Tyler, K.A., D.R. Hoyt, L.B. Whitbeck and A.M. Cauce. 2001. "The Effects of a High Risk Environment on the Sexual Victimization of Homeless and Runaway Youth." *Violence and Victims* 16(4):441–55.

Unger, J., T. Simon, T. Newman, S. Montgomery, M. Kipke and M. Albornoz. 1998. "Early Adolescent Street Youth: An Overlooked Population with Unique Problems." *Journal of Early Adolescence* 18(4):325–48.

United Nations AIDS (UNAIDS). 2001. *Preventing hiv/aids Among Young People*. New York, NY: United Nations.

Van Brunschot, E.G. 1995. "Youth Involvement in Prostitution." In James H. Creechan and Robert A. Silverman, (eds.), *Canadian Delinquency*. Scarborough, ON: Prentice Hall.

van der Kolk, B. A., A.C. McFarlane and L. Weisaeth. 1996. *Traumatic Stress: The Effects of Overwhelming Experience on Mind, Body, and Society*. New York, NY: Guilford.

Vanwesenbeeck, I. 2001. "Another Decade of Social Scientific Work on Sex Work: A Review of Research 1990–2000." *Annual Review of Sex Research.* 12:242–89.

Veale, A., M. Taylor and C. Linehan. 2000. "Psychological Perspectives of 'Abandoned' and 'Abandoning' Children." In C. Panter-Brick and M.T. Smith (eds.), *Abandoned Children*. Cambridge, MA: Cambridge University Press.

Ward, C. 1997. *Havens and Springboards: The Foyer Movement in Context*. London, UK: Calouste Gulbenkian Foundation.

Weinberg, M., F. Shaver and C. Williams. 1999. "Gendered Sex Work in the San Francisco Tenderloin." *Archives of Sexual Behavior* 28:503–21.

Weisberg, D.K. 1985. *Children of the Night: A Study of Adolescent Prostitution*. Lexington, MA: Lexington Books.

Whitbeck, L.B., D.R. Hoyt and D. Yoder. 1999. *Nowhere to Grow: Homeless and Runaway Adolescents and their Families*. Hawthorne, NY: Aldine de Gruyter.

Whitbeck L.B., and D. Simons. 1990. "Life on the Streets: The Victimization of Runaway and Homeless Adolescents." *Youth and Society* 22:108–25.

Young, A., C. Boyd and A. Hubbell. 2000. "Prostitution, Drug Use and Coping with Psychological Distress." *Journal of Drug Issues* 30(4):789–800.

Legislation, Constitutional Documents and International Conventions

Canadian Charter of Rights and Freedoms, Part I of the *Constitutional Act, 1982*, Schedule B to the *Canada Act, 1982*, 1982, U.K., c.11.

Criminal Code, R.S.C. 1985, c.C-46.

International Convention for the Suppression of the Traffic in Women and Children, 9 U.N.T.S. 416. No.269 1922).

See also Appendix to Chapter Five on provincial child protection statutes.

Caselaw

B.H. v. *Alberta (Director of Child Welfare).* 2002. Alberta Judgments No.518 (Q/L) (Court of Queen's Bench); affirmed [2002] Alberta Judgments No. 568 (Court of Appeal); leave to appeal to Supreme Court of Canada denied (July 11, 2002).

Chimiliar v. *Chimiliar.* 2001. Alberta Judgments No.838 (Q/L) (Court of Queen's Bench).

J.C.S. v. *Wren.* 1987. 2 Western Weekly Reports 669 (Alberta Court of Appeal).

K.B. and M.J. v. *Alberta.* 2000. Alberta Judgments No. 876 (Provincial Court) (Q/L), reversed [2000] Alberta Judgments No.1570 (Court of Queen's Bench) (Q/L).

K.L.W. v. *Winnipeg Child and Family Services.* 2000. 2 Supreme Court of Canada Reports 519.

R. v. *Feeney.* 1997. 115 Canadian Criminal Cases (3d) 129 (Supreme Court of Canada).

Winnipeg Child and Family Services v. *G.(D.F.).* 1997. 3 Supreme Court Reports 925.

Also in the Hurting and Healing Series on Intimate Violence
Co-published by Fernwood Publishing and RESOLVE

Reclaiming Self
Issues and Resources for Women Abused by
Intimate Partners
Leslie M. Tutty and Carolyn Goard, eds.
120pp 1 55266 077 X $16.95

This book considers the many aspects of supporting
and providing safety for women who experience
abuse. The authors focus on the impact of government policies, such as the criminal justice response
and child protection services, on a woman's ability to safely leave an
abusive relationship. Each chapter presents the results of recent Canadian
research and documents the voices of women who share their experiences of having been abused by an intimate partner.

Pieces of a Puzzle
Perspectives on Child Sexual Abuse
Diane Hierbert-Murphy and Linda Burnside, eds.
128pp 1 55266 043 5 $16.95

Topics in this collection include treatment for child
victims, grooming patterns of offenders, a family
systems approach to treatment, criminal prosecution
in child sexual abuse cases and the use of community
notification programs.

No Place For Violence
Canadian Aboriginal Alternatives
Jocelyn Proulx and Sharon Perrault eds.
140pp 1 55266 034 6 $16.95

This volume presents a number of studies on the
effects of colonization, the need for programming
specific to and by Aboriginal people and the efforts
made by the Aboriginal community to meet that
need.